PENGUIN PASSNOTES

The Catcher in the Rye

Alan Gardiner was educated at Cambridge and London universities. An examiner in English Literature for several
years, he has taught at various London colleges and is cur-
rently a lecturer in English Language and Literature at
Redbridge Technical College. He is also the author of the
study guides to *Billy Liar* and *Saint Joan* in the Penguin
Passnotes series.

William Bu...

PENGUIN PASSNOTES

J. D. SALINGER

The Catcher in the Rye

ALAN GARDINER

ADVISORY EDITOR: S. H. COOTE M.A., PH.D.

PENGUIN BOOKS

PENGUIN BOOKS

Published by the Penguin Group
27 Wrights Lane, London W8 5TZ, England
Viking Penguin Inc., 40 West 23rd Street, New York, New York 10010, USA
Penguin Books Australia Ltd, Ringwood, Victoria, Australia
Penguin Books Canada Ltd, 2801 John Street, Markham, Ontario, Canada L3R 1B4
Penguin Books (NZ) Ltd, 182–190 Wairau Road, Auckland 10, New Zealand

Penguin Books Ltd, Registered Offices: Harmondsworth, Middlesex, England

First published 1989
10 9 8 7 6 5 4 3 2 1

Made and printed in Great Britain by
Richard Clay Ltd, Bungay, Suffolk
Filmset in Monophoto Ehrhardt

Contents

To the Student

This book is designed to help you with your GCSE English Literature examination. It contains a synopsis of the novel, a glossary of the more unfamiliar words and phrases, and a commentary on some of the issues raised by the text. An account of the writer's life is also included for background.

Page references in parentheses refer to the Penguin edition of J. D. Salinger's *The Catcher in the Rye*.

When you use this book, remember that it is no more than an aid to your study. It will help you find passages quickly and perhaps give you some ideas for essays. But remember also: *This book is not a substitute for reading the novel, and it is your knowledge and your response that matter*. These are the things that the examiners are looking for, and they are also the things that will give you the most pleasure. Show your knowledge and appreciation to the examiner, and show them clearly.

Introduction

When *The Catcher in the Rye* was first published in 1951, it made a dramatic impact upon millions of readers and quickly became a cult success. Young people in Britain, the USA and many other countries readily identified with Holden Caulfield, the novel's seventeen-year-old narrator – with his idealism, his contempt for the hypocrisies of the adult world, his rejection of conformity, his fears and uncertainties about growing up. In the decade that followed, youthful rebellion became a familiar element in British and American culture: in drama, fiction, films and popular music. J. D. Salinger can fairly claim to have initiated this tradition. *The Catcher in the Rye* expressed the restlessness and dissatisfaction of the young in a language they could recognize and understand. In the 1980s the novel has continued to enjoy popularity. Surprisingly, for a work that so successfully captures the mood of its time, *The Catcher in the Rye* has not dated. Holden Caulfield's observations about mid-twentieth-century society remain relevant and telling, and the transition from adolescence to adulthood is a theme that has lost none of its validity.

Jerome David Salinger was thirty-two when *The Catcher in the Rye* was published. It was his first full-length novel (and at the time of writing remains his only one), though he had been writing shorter pieces of fiction for several years. He was born on 1 January 1919, the son of a prosperous New York importer. Like Holden Caulfield, Salinger had an unsettled education. At the age of thirteen he became a pupil at a private school in Manhattan, but he left after a year and entered Valley Forge Military Academy; later he briefly attended New York University and Ursinus College, Pennsylvania. In 1938 he began to study creative writing at Columbia University. The teacher of the course was the editor of a magazine, and in 1940 he published a short story by Salinger, *The Young Folks*. In the next few years Salinger's stories appeared in other magazines, such as *Esquire* and the *Saturday Evening Post*. During this time he also served with the United States Army. In 1943 he was posted to Europe and the following year he took part in the D-Day landings.

After the war Salinger returned to the USA, and in 1948 he signed a contract with the prestigious *New Yorker* magazine, which has published most of his short fiction. *The Catcher in the Rye* brought international recognition of Salinger's talent and established him as one of the most important fiction writers of his time. The novel was also controversial, however; it was banned in some countries and several American states directed that it should not be read in schools and colleges. The bizarre circumstances surrounding the murder of former Beatle John Lennon in New York in 1980 brought further controversy. Lennon's deranged killer, Mark Chapman, had been obsessed with the novel for ten years or more and read aloud from it at his trial. He claimed, 'I am indeed the catcher in the rye of this generation.'

Salinger's published literary output is not extensive. *Nine Stories* (1953) is a collection of pieces that had originally appeared in magazines (most of them in the *New Yorker*). A few of them are about the Glass family, the subject of almost all Salinger's fiction since *The Catcher in the Rye*. Les and Bessie Glass are retired vaudeville entertainers who live in New York. They have seven children: Seymour, Buddy, Walker, Wake, Boo Boo, Franny and Zooey. Other stories in the Glass saga have been published as *Franny and Zooey* (1961) and *Raise High the Roof Beam, Carpenters, and Seymour: An Introduction* (1963). In 1965 another Glass story, *Hapworth 16, 1924*, appeared in the *New Yorker*. Many of the themes in the Glass stories are similar to those of *The Catcher in the Rye*: childhood, human imperfection and the materialism and hypocrisy of contemporary society.

Salinger has apparently written much that he has chosen to leave unpublished. This reluctance to share his work with the reading public has been accompanied by a reclusive personal life. It is in accordance with Salinger's wishes that photographs and biographical details never appear on the jackets of his books, and in the early 1950s he erected a high fence around his home to protect his privacy further. He refuses requests for interviews and in the 1980s took legal action to thwart the efforts of a biographer, the British writer Ian Hamilton.

CHAPTER 2, *pp. 11–19*

Mr Spencer is about seventy years old. He has been in ill health and is sitting wrapped up in a blanket. His room is full of pills and medicine, and Holden finds the scene depressing. Mr Spencer questions Holden about his recent interview with the headmaster, Dr Thurmer, and asks how his parents are likely to react to the news of his expulsion. They then discuss Holden's academic record and Holden admits that English has been his only successful subject. Mr Spencer reads aloud the pitifully short essay Holden wrote for his history examination and asks if he had any choice but to fail him. It emerges that Holden has had trouble settling down at other schools as well. Mr Spencer tries to make him think seriously about his future, but Holden, who has been feeling increasingly restless and uncomfortable, says he has to go.

CHAPTER 3, *pp. 20–30*

Holden returns to his room and has just begun reading when he is interrupted by Robert Ackley, a boy in the same dormitory. Holden is very irritated by Ackley, who continues to pester him until Ward Stradlater, Holden's room-mate, arrives. Ackley does not like Stradlater and leaves soon after. Stradlater is confident, extrovert and rather conceited. He is going out for the evening with a girl (who is waiting for him in the Annex), and he asks Holden if he may borrow his jacket.

CHAPTER 4, *pp. 31–8*

Stradlater goes to the dormitory bathroom to shave and Holden accompanies him. He asks Holden to write an English composition for him, and he also tells Holden that his date is Jane Gallagher, a girl Holden had known well two summers earlier. Holden is excited by this news, but, instead of going downstairs to speak to her, he just asks Stradlater to give her his regards. Having gone back to his room, he sits in his chair thinking about Jane and becomes dejected at the thought of her spending the evening with Stradlater. Ackley barges in uninvited once again, and this time Holden is pleased to see him: 'He took my mind off the other stuff' (p. 38).

CHAPTER 5, *pp. 39–43*

Holden, Ackley and Mal Brossard (another Pencey pupil) catch a bus into Agerstown. They play pinball and eat a few hamburgers and then return to Pencey. Holden writes Stradlater's composition, choosing as his topic a baseball glove that had belonged to his dead brother, Allie. He remembers the glove well because Allie had written poems all over it in green ink. Allie, who was two years younger than Holden, had died of leukaemia in 1946, when Holden was thirteen. Holden had reacted badly to the death and had smashed all the windows in his family's garage.

CHAPTER 6, *pp. 44–9*

When Stradlater returns, Holden is feeling tense and agitated; he has again been worrying about Stradlater and Jane and what might occur between them. Stradlater reads the composition and complains that the subject is unsuitable, so Holden snatches it out of his hand and tears it up. He questions Stradlater about his evening with Jane and ends by attacking him. In the fight that follows Holden comes off worst and is left with his face covered in blood. He goes into the next room to see Ackley.

CHAPTER 7, *pp. 50–56*

Ackley's room-mate is away for the weekend and Holden asks if he may sleep in his bed. Ackley is reluctant to give his permission, which annoys Holden. He lies on top of the bed anyway, and begins thinking about Stradlater and Jane Gallagher again. He is lonely and miserable. After coming out of Ackley's room, he suddenly decides to leave Pencey that night rather than waiting until term officially ends. He will stay at a hotel in New York for a few days and go home on Wednesday, by which time his parents should have had time to digest the news of his expulsion. He packs his bags, sells his typewriter to another pupil for twenty dollars and leaves the building with a loud cry of '*Sleep tight, ya morons!*'

CHAPTER 8, *pp. 57–62*

Holden walks to the railway station. On the train a lady sits next to him and spots the Pencey Prep sticker on one of his bags. She tells Holden that her son, Ernest Morrow, is also a pupil at the school. Holden knows the boy and dislikes him intensely, but he tells Mrs Morrow her son is extremely popular and makes up several stories to support this assertion. When she asks why Holden is going home early, he lies again, saying he has to have an operation to remove a tumour from his brain.

CHAPTER 9, *pp. 63–70*

When he arrives at New York's Penn Station, Holden goes into a phone-booth, but, after thinking of various people he might ring, he leaves without calling any of them. He then goes by taxi to a seedy hotel, where he intends spending the next few days. He soon discovers that the hotel is 'full of perverts and morons' (p. 65). From the window of his room he observes the behaviour of some of the occupants of the rooms opposite. He sees a man dress himself in women's clothing and a couple squirting water out of their mouths at each other. He decides to call Faith Cavendish, a girl whose name and telephone number had been given to him by a youth at a party. Initially she is annoyed at being telephoned so late at night and, although she becomes quite friendly, she says she cannot meet Holden for a cocktail.

CHAPTER 10, *pp. 71–80*

Holden thinks of ringing his ten-year-old sister, Phoebe, but decides not to as one of his parents might answer. His affection for Phoebe is very apparent in his description of her. He goes downstairs to the hotel's Lavender Room, where a band is playing. He is refused an alcoholic drink because of his age and instead has a Coke. At the next table are three women, aged around thirty, who come from Seattle and are visiting New York. He dances with each one in turn, but none of them shows much interest in him; when they go, they leave Holden to pay the sizeable drinks bill.

CHAPTER 11, *pp. 81–5*

Holden sits in the hotel lobby, thinking again about Jane Gallagher. He recalls the summer before last when they spent a lot of time together. He decides to go out and takes a taxi to Ernie's, a nightclub in Greenwich Village.

CHAPTER 12, *pp. 86–92*

Holden has quite a lengthy conversation with the taxi driver on the question of where the ducks in New York's Central Park go during the winter – something that has been puzzling him for some time. At

Ernie's he meets Lillian Simmons, his brother D.B.'s ex-girlfriend, who is with a navy officer. Holden does not want to spend much time in their company so he leaves the club, telling Lillian he has to meet somebody.

CHAPTER 13, *pp. 93–103*

Holden walks back to his hotel. The liftman asks if he wants a prostitute and says it will cost him five dollars. Holden accepts the offer without thinking and almost immediately regrets having done so. As he waits in his room, he is nervous about what he realizes is an opportunity to lose his virginity. When the prostitute arrives, Holden tries to engage her in friendly conversation, but she is restless and impatient. Holden feels increasingly despondent and ill at ease and is unable to bring himself to go to bed with the girl. He says he will pay her anyway and hands her a five-dollar bill. Although she tells Holden she expected ten dollars, he refuses to pay her any more.

CHAPTER 14, *pp. 104–10*

After Sunny, the prostitute, has left, Holden sits in a chair, smoking. He begins to talk out loud, imagining he is speaking to his dead brother, Allie. Eventually he goes to bed. As he describes how he tries to say a prayer and finds he cannot, the reader learns some of his views on religion. Suddenly Holden is startled by a knock on the door. Sunny and Maurice, the liftman, force their way into the room, demanding that Holden pay another five dollars. When Holden refuses to give them any more money, Maurice threatens him. Sunny takes the money from Holden's wallet and he begins crying. He remains defiant, however, and calls Maurice a 'dirty moron' (p. 108). Maurice reacts to this by punching Holden in the stomach. After the departure of Sunny and Maurice, Holden walks with difficulty to the bathroom, where he has a bath before going back to bed, so dispirited he feels like committing suicide.

CHAPTER 15, *pp. 111–19*

In the morning Holden rings a girlfriend, Sally Hayes, whom he finds physically attractive, though he does not like her personality. He arranges to go with her to a theatre that afternoon. He checks out of the hotel and takes a taxi to Grand Central Station to put his bags in a locker. He has breakfast at a sandwich bar and is joined at his table by two nuns. He begins talking to them and learns that they are schoolteachers from Chicago who have come to New York to teach at a convent school. Holden gives them ten dollars as a contribution to their charity collection. One of the nuns is an English teacher, and Holden tells her it is his best subject. They talk about the books he has studied.

CHAPTER 16, *pp. 120–28*

After he leaves the sandwich bar, Holden walks to Broadway, partly because he hopes to buy a record for his sister, Phoebe. On the way he passes a little boy singing 'If a body catch a body coming through the rye'. Holden enjoys watching and listening to the boy and begins to feel less depressed. He finds the record he wants in the first shop he visits. He tries to telephone Jane Gallagher, but hangs up when her mother answers. He buys two tickets for the afternoon performance of a play called *I Know My Love* and then takes a taxi to Central Park. He walks over to a children's skating area where he thinks he might find Phoebe, but she is not there, and he decides to walk through the park to the Museum of Natural History. He recalls that when he was much younger, a schoolteacher used to take his class there on regular visits. Once he arrives at the museum, however, the desire to go inside suddenly disappears. Instead he takes a taxi to the Biltmore Hotel to meet Sally Hayes.

CHAPTER 17, *pp. 129–40*

Holden arrives early at the Biltmore; the lobby is crowded with young girls, and he sits and watches them as he waits for Sally. When Sally arrives, they go to the theatre by taxi. Holden is not a lover of drama and he does not enjoy the play, though he admits he has seen worse. During the interval they meet a young man whom Sally knows. Holden takes an instant dislike to him, finding him conceited and pretentious. After the play is over, Sally suggests they go ice-skating at the Radio City ice-rink. They skate for a while and then go to the rink's bar for a drink. Holden asks Sally if she ever gets fed up, and then, in a long, emotional speech, tells her how much he hates school and living in New York. He says he wants to get away and asks Sally to come with him. He becomes angry when she refuses and ends by insulting her. He tries to apologize, but Sally is annoyed and upset, and Holden leaves the skating-rink alone.

CHAPTER 18, *pp. 141–7*

When Holden tries to telephone Jane, again there is no answer. He then rings Carl Luce, an old schoolfriend who is three years older than Holden. Holden does not like him much, but since he feels in need of company, he arranges to meet Luce in a bar later that evening. To fill in time Holden goes to see a film, and, although he thinks it is terrible, he watches it through to the end. The central character is an Englishman who was wounded in the Second World War, and as Holden walks to the bar where he is to meet Carl Luce, he thinks about wars and how he would feel if he had to fight in one.

CHAPTER 19, *pp. 148–55*

Holden arrives at the Wicker Bar and has two drinks before Luce arrives. Luce is arrogant and affected, but Holden is amused by him and respects his intelligence. Luce seems bored by Holden and becomes irritated when Holden questions him about his sex life. Luce advises Holden to consider a course of psychoanalysis and then tells him he has to leave for another appointment.

CHAPTER 20, *pp. 156–63*

Holden sits drinking by himself in the Wicker Bar until one o'clock in the morning. He makes a drunken telephone call to Sally Hayes and tells her he will go to her house, as arranged, on Christmas Eve to help her trim the Christmas tree. He staggers to the men's room, fills a wash-basin with cold water and plunges his head into it. By the time he goes to the cloakroom to collect his coat he is crying: 'I guess it was because I was feeling so damn depressed and lonesome' (p. 159). He then walks to Central Park, intending to visit the lake and see if any ducks are there. At the park he drops Phoebe's record, which shatters into tiny pieces. He knows the park well, but in his drunken state he has great difficulty finding the lake. When he eventually does, he walks all around it without seeing a single duck. He sits shivering on a bench and becomes afraid that he is going to catch pneumonia and die. He imagines how his family would react to his death and decides he ought to see Phoebe before anything happens to him. He leaves the park and walks to his home.

CHAPTER 21, *pp. 164–72*

Holden slips quietly into his family's apartment and creeps first to Phoebe's room and then to his brother's room, where Phoebe sleeps when D.B. is away from home. Holden reads through one of her notebooks before waking Phoebe, who is excited to see him and explains that her parents are out at a party. Phoebe wonders why Holden is home before the school term has finished and guesses that he has been expelled. This angers and upsets her and she buries her head in her pillow.

CHAPTER 22, *pp. 173–80*

Phoebe asks Holden why he was expelled from Pencey. He tries to
explain what he disliked about the school. When Phoebe asks what he
does like, he says he liked their brother Allie and likes what he is doing
now, sitting talking to Phoebe. He then refers to the song he heard
the little boy singing (in Chapter 16), 'If a body catch a body comin''
through the rye', and tells Phoebe he has a picture in his mind of
a large group of children playing in a field of rye near the edge of a
cliff. What he would really like to be is a person standing at the top
of the cliff catching the children if they run too close to the edge –
the catcher in the rye. He thinks of telephoning Mr Antolini, an
English teacher at one of his previous schools, and leaves the bedroom
to make the call.

CHAPTER 23, *pp. 181–7*

Holden tells Mr Antolini, whom he regards as the best teacher he has
ever had, that he has been expelled from Pencey, and Mr Antolini
says he may come over to his apartment straight away. When Holden
returns to the bedroom, the radio is playing, and he and Phoebe
dance to the music for a while. Their parents return and Holden
quickly hides himself in a cupboard. He hears their mother come into
the room and speak to Phoebe. After she has gone, Holden asks
Phoebe if she can lend him any money – he has none left. When
Phoebe insists that he take the money she has saved for Christmas, he
begins to cry. Finally he leaves, promising Phoebe he will try to
contact her before he returns home on Wednesday.

CHAPTER 24, *pp. 188–200*

Holden goes to the expensive apartment shared by Mr Antolini and
his wife. The couple have given a party that night, and Holden notices

that Mr Antolini is a little drunk. Mrs Antolini makes some coffee for Holden and then goes to bed. Her husband talks to Holden about his experiences at Pencey. He is worried by Holden's apparent aimlessness and disillusionment with life. He tells Holden he needs to find some direction and to recognize the benefits to be gained from taking his education more seriously. Holden is tired and cannot stop himself yawning. The two of them make up a bed on the couch and when Holden lies down, he goes to sleep almost immediately. Suddenly he is wakened by a strange sensation and discovers Mr Antolini stroking his hair. He leaps from the couch, dresses as quickly as he can and tells Mr Antolini he has to collect his bags from Grand Central Station.

CHAPTER 25, *pp. 201–19*

Holden goes to Grand Central Station and sleeps on a bench there for a few hours. After leaving the station, he walks along Fifth Avenue, which is crowded with Christmas shoppers. He is feeling decidedly unwell – he is sweating, nauseous and has a headache. He decides he will leave New York and hitch-hike to the West, where he will work until he can afford to buy himself a cabin. He wants to say goodbye to Phoebe before going so he walks to her school and hands a note to a secretary asking Phoebe to meet him at the Museum of Art at lunchtime. When Phoebe arrives, she is carrying a large suitcase. She tells Holden she intends to go away with him and has been home to pack her clothes. Holden speaks to her very sternly and says she cannot accompany him. Phoebe starts to cry. Holden then says he has changed his mind and will not be going away. He offers to walk with Phoebe back to her school, but she refuses to move. When he asks if she wants to go to the zoo, she gives no reply. Holden begins walking to the zoo and Phoebe follows him at a distance. As they look at the animals, Phoebe is still sullen. She softens towards Holden, however, when they go to the roundabout in the park. Phoebe rides on it and Holden sits on a bench watching her. He suddenly feels very happy and remains on the bench in spite of being drenched by a heavy downpour of rain.

CHAPTER 26, *p. 220*

Holden says that he will not describe in detail what took place after he left the park. The reader learns, however, that he became ill and is at present in a hospital, that his treatment includes sessions with a psychoanalyst and that in September he is meant to be starting at a new school. Holden concludes by saying that the telling of his story has made him miss everybody mentioned in it – even people such as Ackley and Maurice, the liftman.

Commentary

CHAPTER 1, *pp.* 5–10

From the opening sentence of the novel Holden Caulfield, the narrator, speaks in the authentic voice of an American teenager: 'If you really want to hear about it, the first thing you'll probably want to know is where I was born, and what my lousy childhood was like, and how my parents were occupied and all before they had me, and all that David Copperfield kind of crap, but I don't feel like going into it' (p. 5). His tone is direct ('If you really want to hear about it'), forceful ('I don't feel like going into it') and conversational ('lousy', 'and all', 'all that David Copperfield kind of crap'). Holden's brisk, vigorous delivery succeeds in retaining our attention, while his familiarity encourages us to feel close to him and to see the world through his eyes.

In the sentence just quoted Holden makes it immediately clear that this will not be a conventional life story. He is not going to begin with a description of his parents and then give a chronological account of his life, starting with his birth and moving on to his childhood. Instead his narrative will concentrate on just a few days from his recent past, telling the story of the 'madman stuff' that happened to him 'around last Christmas' (p. 5). While this brief period of time provides the framework for the novel, Holden continually reaches back into the more distant past to recall people, places and experiences, so that by the close of the book the reader will have gained an intimate and comprehensive knowledge of his character. The kind of information that is normally included in an autobiography is not presented in a conventional form, but it emerges none the less. In the opening paragraph, for example, Holden talks a little about his parents and his brother. It is evident that at the time of writing Holden is living not at home but somewhere near Hollywood, and has gone there to rest. Later in the chapter it becomes clearer that he is in some kind of hospital (p. 9).

One of Holden's most important characteristics to emerge in this chapter is his dislike of 'phoniness'. He has a deep respect for honesty and truth and is quick to spot pretence, hypocrisy or fraud. He is contemptuous of his brother D.B. because he has abandoned the writing of books – for which he had a genuine gift – in order to make money: he has become a 'prostitute', selling his talent to the Hollywood film industry (p. 5). Pencey Prep, the school Holden last attended (and which he is about to leave at the time his story begins), is another example of phoniness. Advertisements for the school depict a young man on a horse, with the caption 'Since 1888 we have been moulding boys into splendid, clear-thinking young men' (p. 6). Holden comments scathingly that he has never seen a horse anywhere near the school and can only think of two people there who might be described as splendid and clear-thinking – 'And they probably *came* to Pencey that way' (p. 6).

Holden's dislike of Pencey Prep helps to explain his poor academic record there. His narrative begins on the last Saturday of term, and he admits that he is leaving because he has been expelled. He had been given frequent warnings about his lack of effort and was failing in four of his five subjects (p. 7). Holden has been unable to enter into the life of the school in the way that is expected of him, because he cannot accept its attitudes and values. It is appropriate that during the football game against Saxon Hall ('It was the last game of the year, and you were supposed to commit suicide or something if old Pencey didn't win', p. 6), Holden is not in the grandstand with the rest of the boys but standing by himself on the top of a hill, watching the game from a distance. In the next chapter the reader learns that Holden has had difficulties settling at other schools, and as the novel continues it becomes clear that his attitude towards society as a whole is marked by a similar detachment and refusal to conform.

Although he feels no real affection or loyalty towards Pencey Prep, Holden believes he should experience some emotion at leaving the school; as he stands on the hill, he is 'trying to feel some kind of a goodbye' (p. 8). This reveals his sensitivity, a quality that is also evident in his dealings with other people. He meets very few people whom he can love, trust or respect, yet his manner towards others is usually warm and open. He is particularly kindhearted to those who are lonely, unhappy or unsuccessful. His attitude to Selma Thurmer, the headmaster's daughter, illustrates this. She is physically unattractive – 'She had a big nose and her nails were all bitten down and bleedy-looking' – but Holden 'felt sort of sorry for her' (p. 7). He is also impressed by her honesty: when they met, she did not speak admiringly of her father, and he thinks this was probably because she shared Holden's low opinion of him.

CHAPTER 2, *pp. 11–19*

Holden visits his history teacher, Mr Spencer, to say goodbye before he leaves Pencey Prep. Mr Spencer is a kind man who takes a genuine interest in his pupils. He and his wife regularly invite Pencey students to their house. He tries to convince Holden that his poor academic performance is a matter for serious concern and asks whether he has given any thought to his future. His advice is well intentioned, though he humiliates Holden unnecessarily when he reads aloud his history examination paper.

In calling on Mr Spencer Holden displays his consideration for others, one of his most appealing characteristics. He asks Mr Spencer (who has been ill) about his health and remains polite and respectful throughout their conversation, even when Mr Spencer rebukes him for his examination results and his failure to think seriously about his future. When he is asked if he ever read his history textbook, Holden claims to have glanced through it a few times as he does not want to hurt Mr Spencer's feelings (p. 15). Shaking hands with Mr Spencer before leaving makes him feel 'sad as hell' (p. 19). He puts his hand on Mr Spencer's shoulder and reassures him that he will be all right: 'Please don't worry about me' (p. 19).

In the course of the conversation, however, it has become increasingly clear that Holden and Mr Spencer are unable to communicate. Holden grows more and more restless and gets up to leave: 'I couldn't've sat there another ten minutes to save my life' (p. 19). Mr Spencer adheres to the conventional values of school and society and, in encouraging Holden to plan for the future and to take his academic studies more seriously, he is trying to persuade him to share these values. As was apparent in the previous chapter, Holden feels alienated from Pencey Prep, and the rest of the novel will show that he feels alienated from society as a whole. He and Mr Spencer have totally different outlooks, and Holden sums up the division between them when he observes, 'we were too much on opposite sides of the pole' (p. 19).

Mr Spencer's old age and sickness create another barrier between them. To Holden Mr Spencer's physical decrepitude is such that 'you wondered what the heck he was still living for' (p. 11). His body is bent forward, and if he dropped a piece of chalk in class, someone had to pick it up for him. When Holden visits him, he is wearing a bathrobe, and Holden finds the way he looks distasteful. He admits to the reader that he is always repelled by old men's bodies, by their bumpy chests and their white, unhairy legs. Holden is also depressed by the pervasive atmosphere of illness in Mr Spencer's room – the smell of Vicks' Nose Drops, the pills and medicine scattered around – and says he is 'not too crazy about sick people' (p. 11). Holden's attitude to Mr Spencer illustrates the difficulty he has in coming to terms with the realities of adult life, which include old age and physical decline.

As mentioned in the discussion of the previous chapter, Holden's dislike of phoniness is one of the novel's most important themes. It is seen here in his comments on Elkton Hills, one of his previous schools. He reveals that one of his main reasons for leaving the school was that he 'was surrounded by phonies' (p. 18). He singles out for particular criticism the headmaster, Mr Haas, who would speak ingratiatingly and at great length to visiting parents who appeared successful and fashionable but ignore others. Mr Spencer suggests that Holden has had 'some difficulty' at other schools he has attended (p. 17). The reluctance to conform he has displayed at Pencey Prep has evidently caused Holden problems in the past.

During his talk with Mr Spencer Holden finds himself thinking about the ducks that live on a lagoon in Central Park in New York (p. 17) and wondering where they go in winter when the lagoon ices over. This problem worries Holden, and he returns to it several times in the course of the novel. His anxiety over the ducks may be seen to reflect his concern for those who appear to be vulnerable and in need of protection. It is certainly a problem the harsh adult world has no time for, as is clear when Holden attempts to discuss it with New York taxi drivers in Chapters 9 and 12.

CHAPTER 3, *pp. 20–30*

After he leaves Mr Spencer's house, Holden goes to his room in the Ossenburger Memorial Wing of the school dormitories. The wing is named after one of Pencey's old boys, who had visited the school earlier in the year and given a speech to the boys. Holden has a very low opinion of Ossenburger, regarding him as a cynical businessman and another phoney. He is an undertaker, and Holden speaks disapprovingly of the fortune he has made from offering cut-price burials: 'He probably just shoves them in a sack and dumps them in the river' (p. 20). He also comments on the insincerity of Ossenburger's speech to the school. He began by telling some jokes, 'to show us what a regular guy he was' (p. 20), and then told the boys they should always pray to God, regardless of where they were. He thought of Jesus as a friend and talked to him when he was driving his car. Holden observes contemptuously, 'I can just see the big phoney bastard shifting into first gear and asking Jesus to send him a few more stiffs' (pp. 20–21).

In his room Holden reads a book he has borrowed from the school library. He tells the reader about some of the authors he likes, saying that he most admires writers who make him wish they were friends of his, people he would like to chat to on the telephone. In narrating his own story Holden adopts a friendly approach to the reader and a relaxed, informal tone. The colloquial and loosely structured narrative style of one of his favourite authors, the American writer Ring Lardner, is very similar to that of *The Catcher in the Rye*.

Soon after he has begun reading, Holden is interrupted by Robert Ackley, a fellow pupil at Pencey whose room is next to Holden's. Ackley is a social misfit who is unpopular with the other boys at the school. He never brushes his teeth, his face is covered with pimples and in the company of others he is awkward and insensitive. Ackley ignores much of what Holden says and continues to pester him even though he can see Holden is trying to read his book. He picks up and moves around Holden's and Stradlater's possessions and sits on the arm of Stradlater's chair, cutting his fingernails and allowing the clippings to fall on the floor. Holden is irritated and disgusted by Ackley's behaviour, but he also feels sorry for him. He tries to convince him that Stradlater had a point when he remarked that Ackley should begin brushing his teeth: 'All he meant was you'd look better and *feel* better' (p. 28).

Ackley leaves when Stradlater, whom he dislikes, enters the room. Stradlater has a date with a girl that evening and asks Holden if he may borrow his hound's-tooth jacket. An energetic character, he 'was always in a big hurry' (p. 29); he is vain and self-centred but is also good-natured, as shown by his friendly greeting to Ackley. He is older than Holden, who rather envies his maturity and masculinity and comments on his 'heavy beard' (p. 29) and 'damn good build' (p. 30).

CHAPTER 4, *pp. 31–8*

Holden joins Stradlater in the dormitory bathroom, where he has gone to shave. Stradlater's vanity is evident in his preparations to go out for the evening. He shaves himself twice 'to look gorgeous' (p. 34) and spends a great deal of time combing his hair. Holden remarks, 'The reason he fixed himself up to look good was because he was madly in love with himself' (p. 31). His self-centredness is such that he does not listen to much of what Holden says. More appealing attributes are his relaxed, carefree manner and his sense of humour; he laughs when Holden tap-dances as if he were a character in a film musical (p. 33).

The most important part of the conversation between Holden and Stradlater is that in which they discuss Jane Gallagher. She means a great deal to Holden, and his thoughts turn to her frequently in the course of the novel. He had spent a lot of time in her company two summers ago when her family had been neighbours of the Caulfields'. Stradlater's announcement that she is his date for that evening produces a dramatic reaction in Holden: 'I damn near dropped dead' (p. 35). From what Holden tells Stradlater the reader may gather that his relationship with Jane had been childlike and innocent: their favourite activity together was playing checkers. He also says that Jane had 'a lousy childhood' (p. 36): her parents were divorced and her stepfather was a drunkard who wandered round the house naked in front of Jane. Both these factors are significant and help to explain why Jane means so much to Holden. He values innocence and purity and still likes to think of Jane as an uncorrupted child; and he feels sympathetic and protective towards those who are vulnerable or unhappy.

These two elements in Holden's attitude to Jane also account for his response to the prospect of her spending an evening with Stradlater. In Holden's eyes Jane's purity is threatened by Stradlater, who he believes is sexually experienced: 'I kept thinking about Jane, and about Stradlater having a date with her and all. It made me so nervous I nearly went crazy. I already told you what a sexy bastard Stradlater was' (p. 38). When Stradlater complains that Jane has only signed out from her boarding school until 9.30, Holden's protective instincts are aroused and he becomes angry (p. 38). He is deeply distressed after Stradlater has gone, and Ackley's entrance into the room for once comes as a welcome relief.

CHAPTER 5, *pp. 39–43*

Holden returns to one of the recurring themes of these early chapters, the phoniness of Pencey Prep. On Saturdays the boys at the school are always given steak for their evening meal. Holden is convinced this is done in order to impress parents who visit their children on Sundays and ask what they had for dinner the previous night. 'What a racket,' observes Holden (p. 39). The steak itself, of course, is barely edible.

Holden and a friend of his, Mal Brossard, plan to go to nearby Agerstown for the evening. Out of pity for Ackley, who usually spends Saturday nights on his own, Holden invites him to join them. Ackley is characteristically ungrateful and acts as though he is doing Holden and Brossard a favour by accompanying them. At the close of the chapter, after the boys have returned to the dormitory, Holden listens to Ackley snoring, and his compassionate nature is again evident in his thoughts: 'That guy had just about everything. Sinus trouble, pimples, lousy teeth, halitosis, crumby fingernails. You had to feel a little sorry for the crazy sonuvabitch' (p. 43).

In Agerstown Holden and his friends pass an aimless, uneventful evening; they have some hamburgers, play pinball and catch the bus back to Pencey. When he returns to his room, Holden settles down to begin Stradlater's composition (p. 41). Stradlater had asked him to write about something 'descriptive. A room. Or a house' (p. 32). Holden finds these subjects uninspiring and decides instead to write about Allie's baseball glove. Allie was two years younger than Holden and had died of leukaemia at the age of eleven. His glove was covered in poems so that when he was playing baseball, he had something to read during lulls in the game. As Holden describes this glove, he reflects upon Allie and his early death. It becomes clear to the reader that Allie's death was a formative influence on Holden's development, one that helps to explain his loneliness, melancholy and general dis-illusionment with life. Its impact upon him is evident in his violent reaction at the time: he broke all the windows of his family's garage with his fist. Holden sees Allie's death as a tragic and unjust waste. He was 'the most intelligent member in the family' and 'also the nicest, in lots of ways' (p. 42). He never showed anger towards any-one and when he found something funny, he would laugh so hard 'he just about fell off his chair' (p. 42). Allie's goodness stands in contrast to the cruelty and deceit Holden encounters in his dealings with the adult world. It is significant that Allie died while still a child; as with Jane Gallagher, Holden thinks of him as pure and uncorrupted.

CHAPTER 6, *pp. 44–9*

Holden grows increasingly anxious as he waits for Stradlater to return from his date with Jane Gallagher. To Holden Jane is still the innocent child he played checkers with two summers ago (it does not seem to occur to him that she is now older), and he is fearful of what might happen when she is with Stradlater, who, according to Holden, is 'unscrupulous' where girls are concerned (p. 44).

Stradlater arrives and as he undresses, he asks Holden if he has written his composition. When he reads it, he complains that it is not the kind of composition he had asked Holden to write: 'For Chrissake, Holden. This is about a goddam baseball glove' (p. 45). Holden is already in a tense, hostile mood because of Stradlater's date with Jane Gallagher, and when Stradlater insults by implication someone else he cares for (Allie), he reacts angrily, grabbing the composition and tearing it to pieces. Holden then lies on his bed and begins smoking, deliberately provoking Stradlater, who does not like him breaking the dormitory rules. He questions Stradlater about his evening with Jane. Stradlater antagonizes Holden further when he asks, 'What the hell ya think we did all night – play checkers, for Chrissake?' (p. 46). Eventually Holden, his voice 'shaking something awful', asks if Stradlater and Jane made love (p. 47). Stradlater's flippant reply ('That's a professional secret, buddy') triggers an explosive reaction from Holden, who leaps from his bed and tries to punch Stradlater in the face. Stradlater is older, stronger and fitter than Holden and easily forces him to the ground. Holden continues insulting Stradlater all the time he is pinned down and does so again when Stradlater releases him. Holden is finally knocked to the floor and remains there until Stradlater leaves the room. On looking in the mirror he finds that his face is covered with blood.

The ferocity of Holden's attack on his room-mate indicates the extent of his concern for Jane Gallagher and the strength of his desire that she should not be corrupted by the sexually experienced Stradlater. But there is an element of jealousy in Holden's hostility as well as envy of Stradlater's sexual confidence. The offhand, dismissive way in which Stradlater speaks of Jane is unpleasant, but Holden's physical assault and verbal abuse are undeserved. During the fight itself Stradlater, who knows Holden is no match for him, shows considerable self-restraint; rather than inflict further physical punishment on Holden, he repeatedly tries to calm him down.

CHAPTER 7, *pp. 50–56*

Holden leaves his room and goes into Ackley's. He still cannot remove from his mind the thought of Stradlater and Jane Gallagher together: 'It just drove me stark staring mad when I thought about her and Stradlater parked somewhere in that fat-assed Ed Banky's car. Every time I thought about it, I felt like jumping out the window' (p. 52). He had once double-dated with Stradlater and this increases still further his fear over what might have taken place. He recalls sitting in the front seat of a car and listening while Stradlater, in the back with his date, exercised his seductive charm. He derives no consolation from talking to Ackley, who will not let Holden sleep in his room-mate's bed.

Holden feels lonely and sad, and his frustration with life is such that he briefly toys with the idea of joining a monastery (p. 53). (A similar desire to escape from society is felt by Holden at other points in the novel; later he considers living in a cabin in the woods, for example.) For the time being he contents himself with escaping from Pencey. His decision to leave the school four days early is character-istically impulsive. He does not wait until the morning but packs his bags and goes immediately, pausing only to sell his typewriter and to take a last look down the dormitory corridor. Holden's sensitivity is evident in his regret as he packs the new pair of ice-skates his mother had sent him a few days previously (p. 55). He knows how disap-pointed she will be when she learns that he has been expelled and feels guilty when he thinks of how he has repaid her kindness. His emotional nature is again apparent when he finds himself weeping as he looks at the dormitory for the last time (p. 56). He has been unhappy at the school and has little regard for the teachers or his fellow pupils, but walking out of the school for the last time is still a moving experience for him. However, the tougher, rebellious element in Holden's character reasserts itself in his final cry: '*Sleep tight, ya morons!*' (p. 56).

CHAPTER 8, *pp. 57–62*

Holden catches a train to New York, where he plans to stay in a hotel
before returning home on Wednesday. A middle-aged woman sits
next to him on the train and when she sees the Pencey sticker on one
of his bags, she introduces herself as the mother of one of Holden's
fellow pupils, Ernest Morrow. Holden considers Mrs Morrow very
good-looking and is attracted by her 'terrifically nice smile' (p. 59)
and her charming manner: 'She had quite a lot of sex appeal' (p. 60).
Holden flirts with her in a gentle, innocent way, offering her a
cigarette and inviting her to join him for a cocktail in another part of
the train. It is worth noting that Mrs Morrow is many years older
than Holden and unlikely to respond to his advances. In romantic
encounters with girls closer to his own age Holden is more hesitant
and unsure of himself. Mrs Morrow's attitude towards him is warm
and motherly and he feels safe in her presence.

   In his conversation with Mrs Morrow Holden tells a series of lies:
he changes his name to that of the janitor of his dormitory, he claims
that her son is a shy, modest and popular pupil (whereas in fact
Holden thinks he is a 'rat') and he says that he is leaving Pencey early
because he has to have an operation to remove a tumour from his
brain. This series of increasingly elaborate falsehoods supports
Holden's earlier assertion that he is something of a compulsive liar (p.
20). There are a number of explanations for this aspect of Holden's
character, one of which is that he enjoys exercising his imagination
and indulging in wild flights of fantasy. As he talks to Mrs Morrow
about her son, he gives a detailed, completely fictitious account of an
election for class president in which Ernest was everyone's first choice
but out of modesty refused to stand. It amuses Holden to describe
Ernest as 'a very sensitive boy' when in reality 'that guy Morrow was
about as sensitive as a goddam toilet seat' (p. 59). At the same time
Holden often tells lies to comfort people or to avoid hurting them.
Instead of telling Mrs Morrow the truth about her son, he tells her
what he knows will please her. He believes Ernest Morrow's character
is unlikely to change as he grows older, but he hopes Mrs Morrow
will continue to think of her son as a 'very shy, modest guy that
wouldn't let us nominate him for president' (p. 61). This leads to the
final and most important reason for Holden's lies. They are yet

another indication of the extent of his disappointment with the real world. He finds life depressing and his lies result from a desire to change it.

CHAPTER 9, *pp. 63–70*

Although Holden had wanted to get away from Pencey Prep, once he reaches New York he feels lonely and in need of human contact. He stands in a telephone-booth for twenty minutes and thinks of different people he might call, but for a variety of reasons he rings none of them. One is Sally Hayes, a girl he has spent some time with in the past and who is to appear later in the novel. He rejects the idea because he is afraid her mother will answer, but it is clear that Holden anyway has mixed feelings about Sally; he dislikes the element of insincerity in her character, referring to the 'long, phoney letter' she has written inviting him to help trim her family's Christmas tree on Christmas Eve (p. 63).

On his way to the Edmont Hotel Holden's loneliness is again apparent as he tries to engage the taxi driver in conversation, even inviting him to join him for a cocktail. The driver, however, is cold and uncommunicative.

Holden checks in at the Edmont, which, it transpires, is 'full of perverts and morons' (p. 65). In this and subsequent chapters Holden is seen in a range of New York locations – hotels, bars, nightclubs – which are frequently depicted as seedy and degenerate. They symbolize the reality of adult life, at least as it appears to Holden. His first encounter with the corrupt behaviour of his elders occurs when he looks out of his window and observes the occupants of some of the other rooms. He sees one man change into women's clothing, while in another room a couple were squirting water, or possibly alcohol, out of their mouths at each other.

Describing the behaviour of these people leads Holden to digress on the subject of sex. He admits that his feelings on the topic are confused: 'Sex is something I just don't understand' (p. 67). He is, for example, both fascinated and disgusted by what he has seen taking place in the other hotel rooms. The girl who was having water squirted over her was good-looking, and Holden can see how what she and her partner were doing 'might be quite a lot of fun' (p. 66). But at the same time he finds the activity degrading and offensive (p. 66):

The thing is, though, I don't *like* the idea. It stinks, if you analyse it. I think, if you don't really like a girl, you shouldn't horse around with her at all, and if you *do* like her, then you're supposed to like her face, and if you like her face, then you ought to be careful about doing crumby stuff to it, like squirting water all over it.

Holden believes genuine respect and affection must be part of any sexual relationship, and this explains his self-imposed resolution to stop 'horsing around' with girls he does not like (p. 66). His physical desires and sexual curiosity are too strong, however, and he admits he broke this rule on the very day it was made.

He goes on to betray his own principles again when he telephones Faith Cavendish. Holden was given her telephone number by someone at a party and was told she had been a striptease artist and was sexually promiscuous. When she answers, she is angry at being telephoned late at night by a complete stranger. Her manner changes, however, when Holden mentions Princeton in connection with the youth who gave him her telephone number and implies he too is studying there. She becomes more friendly and begins to speak in a more refined accent. Nevertheless she is not willing to leave her apartment and meet Holden for a cocktail, saying it is too late; she suspects that Holden is very young and is not impressed when he says he is calling from a telephone-booth. Her rejection of Holden's invitation is polite and understandable, but the change in her attitude when Princeton is mentioned suggests she is another 'phoney'. She speaks respectfully to Holden only when she believes he may be a person of wealth and social importance.

CHAPTER 10, *pp. 71–80*

Holden breaks off from his main narrative to give a detailed description of his ten-year-old sister, Phoebe. He has great affection for her and is proud of her intelligence and her prettiness: 'You never saw a little kid so pretty and smart in your whole life' (p. 71). Holden's relationships with adults and with his peers are generally marked by a failure to communicate, but he enjoys an easy rapport with Phoebe. He regards her as 'somebody with sense and all' (p. 71) and states, 'if you tell old Phoebe something, she knows exactly what the hell you're talking about' (p. 72). She shares many of Holden's attitudes and tastes, as is illustrated by her response to films: 'If you take her to a lousy movie, for instance, she knows it's a lousy movie. If you take her to a pretty good movie, she knows it's a pretty good movie' (p. 72). She has a number of endearing, childish habits, such as mimicking the dialogue and action of *The Thirty-Nine Steps* (her favourite film) and writing stories about a girl detective called Hazle Weatherfield. Holden's attitude to Phoebe confirms that he values the innocence of children and that he feels out of place in the adult world. So far in the novel the characters who have come closest to satisfying Holden's need for companionship and love have both been younger than he is — Phoebe and Allie.

After changing in his room, Holden goes downstairs and then into the hotel's Lavender Room where a band is playing. He is again in an environment from which he feels alienated. There is nobody else there of his own age, and his youthfulness is emphasized when a waiter refuses to serve him an alcoholic drink. Three women, aged about thirty, are sitting at a nearby table, and Holden dances with one of them, a blonde named Bernice. He is impressed by her confident, skilful dancing, but his attempts to hold a conversation with her are disastrous. She appears not to listen to much of what he says, is offended by some of his language and objects when he tries to kiss her. The only time she shows any enthusiasm is when she tells Holden that she and her friends had seen a film actor, Peter Lorre, buying a newspaper the previous evening. After hearing this 'very dumb remark', Holden decides Bernice is a 'moron' (p. 76). When he and Bernice have finished dancing, he is not invited to join the girls at their table, but does so anyway. His attempts to engage the other two girls in conversation make little headway. He learns that they are visiting New York and concludes, when they spend much of their time looking around the room (rather than at him), that they are hoping to see film stars. His theory appears to be confirmed when he gets an excited response from one of the girls by telling her that he has just seen Gary Cooper leaving the club. The final sour note is struck when the girls suddenly stand up and say they have to go, leaving Holden to pay their entire drinks bill.

Holden's evening with the three girls from Seattle represents another rejection by adult society and is another disheartening experience. The girls are in awe of those who are famous but are dismissive in their attitude towards Holden. The episode shows that when others fail to meet Holden's hopes and expectations, his judgement of them can be very harsh: he is contemptuous of the girls' sycophantic attitude to film stars, their bad manners and their lack of intelligence.

CHAPTER 11, *pp. 81–5*

When Holden leaves the Lavender Room, he again finds himself thinking of Jane Gallagher, and most of this chapter is devoted to his memories of their relationship. Holden enjoyed Jane's company as well as finding her physically attractive. They spent their time together playing checkers, tennis and golf and going to see films. That Holden felt especially close to Jane is indicated by the fact that she is the only person outside his family to whom he has ever shown Allie's baseball mitt. He talked to her a lot about Allie and she was a sympathetic listener: 'She was interested in that kind of stuff' (p. 82). He did not find Jane quite so open about her own problems, however. One day when they were sitting on Jane's front porch, her drunken stepfather came out of the house and asked where he could find some cigarettes. Jane ignored him, but she began to cry after he had gone back inside. When Holden tried to comfort her, she would not reveal what was wrong. He was saddened by her unhappiness then (he suspected that her stepfather had tried to molest her), and it is clear that he still feels protective towards her. Holden's relationship with Jane had been sexually innocent and they 'never necked or horsed around much' (p. 84), even though he was attracted to her. Generally the only form of physical contact between them was holding hands, which seems to have been enough for Holden: 'You never even worried, with Jane, whether your hand was sweaty or not. All you knew was, you were happy. You really were' (p. 84).

Holden's account of his relationship with Jane Gallagher illustrates his tenderness towards those who are sad and vulnerable. It also offers further evidence that his highest regard is for those who are childlike and innocent. He seems to think adulthood and sexuality are corruptive and values the purity of his friendship with Jane.

At the close of the chapter Holden takes a taxi to Ernie's, a nightclub in Greenwich Village. Ernie is a very good pianist, but he is another character whose attitude to people is influenced by the degree of social prestige they possess: 'He's a terrific snob and he won't hardly even talk to you unless you're a big shot or a celebrity' (p. 85).

CHAPTER 12, *pp. 86–92*

In the taxi Holden again tries to strike up a conversation with the driver. As previously (Chapter 9), he asks the driver where the ducks in Central Park go during the winter. This driver, a man named Horwitz, is more talkative than the first one, but he too is perplexed by Holden's question about the ducks: 'How the hell should I know? . . . How the hell should I know a stupid thing like that?' (p. 87). He changes the subject to fish and claims they are able to survive frozen into one position for the whole winter. Although his manner is so antagonistic that Holden decides 'it wasn't any pleasure discussing anything with him' (p. 88), Holden finds him amusing and invites him to stop off and join him for a drink. Predictably, Horwitz declines.

Unlike the Lavender Room, Ernie's is crowded with people close to Holden's age and from a similarly affluent social background. Nevertheless Holden feels just as alienated: 'I was surrounded by jerks' (p. 90). He is particularly scornful of the crowd's adulatory response to Ernie's piano playing. He sees their reverential attitude as exaggerated and affected: 'It was supposed to be something *holy*, for God's sake, when he sat down at the piano. Nobody's *that* good' (p. 88). When Ernie was finished, 'everybody was clapping their heads off', and Holden observes, 'They were exactly the same morons that laugh like hyenas in the movies at stuff that isn't funny' (p. 89). Ernie himself is another phoney, giving an insincere, humble bow at the end of his performance.

In the club Holden is greeted effusively by Lillian Simmons, an ex-girlfriend of D.B.'s. He considers her 'strictly a phoney' (p. 91) and believes that she is interested only in D.B. and is friendly to Holden because she hopes he will tell D.B. about it. She introduces her companion, a navy officer, and he too appears false, giving an excessively firm handshake to prove that he is tough. When Holden is invited to join the couple, he says he has to leave. 'I certainly wasn't going to sit down at a table with old Lillian Simmons and that Navy guy and be bored to death' (p. 92).

Since his arrival in New York Holden has had a series of encounters with others, yet so far he has met no one he can identify with, no one with whom he can communicate on the basis of shared attitudes and values. He has been unable to establish the kind of rapport he has with Phoebe (and had with Allie and Jane Gallagher). This is partly because people have rejected his attempts at friendship, but, as the meeting with Lillian Simmons illustrates, it is also because he is extremely critical of others. He loathes snobbery, insincerity and unthinking social conformity and is quick – perhaps too quick – to condemn those who are in any way guilty of these failings.

CHAPTER 13, *pp. 93–103*

As Holden describes his walk back to the hotel, he again digresses, telling the reader about his cowardice; he hates fist fights and always tries to avoid physical confrontations. He says that he is 'one of these very yellow guys' (p. 93), but the impression is given that his aversion to fights stems rather from a reluctance to inflict physical pain: 'what scares me most in a fist fight is the guy's face. I can't stand looking at the other guy's face, is my trouble' (pp. 94–5).

When Holden takes the lift to his room, the liftman asks him if he wants the services of a prostitute. Holden impulsively says that he does, but almost immediately regrets his decision. He goes to his room and waits nervously for the prostitute to arrive. Holden confesses to the reader that he is a virgin, and it becomes clear that much of Holden's confusion over the question of sex arises from his inexperience. He claims that he has had several opportunities to lose his virginity, but he did not exploit them, partly because he lacks Stradlater's unscrupulousness. If he is close to making love to a girl and she tells him to stop, he does so: 'The trouble is I get to feeling sorry for them' (p. 97). Holden is anxious to acquire some sexual experience and as he changes into a clean shirt, he tells himself the imminent encounter with a prostitute is his 'big chance' (p. 97).

The prostitute, who says her name is Sunny, is cold and unfriendly. She has a bored, businesslike approach and does not want to waste time talking; despite this air of experience, which contrasts with Holden's apprehensiveness, she is very young. Holden believes she is about his own age and when she responds to his claim that he is twenty-two by saying, 'Like fun you are', he observes that she sounded more like a 'real kid' than a prostitute (p. 99).

Holden cannot bring himself to go to bed with the girl. One reason for this is simply his nervousness. He attempts to appear mature and confident, lying about his age and identifying himself as 'Jim Steele', but his nonchalance is strained and unconvincing. More importantly, he cannot enter into a sexual relationship that is devoid of warmth and love. Before Sunny arrived, Holden had been able to take a detached approach to what was about to take place: 'I figured if she was a prostitute and all, I could get in some practice on her, in case I ever get married or anything' (p. 97). Once he meets her, however, it is impossible for him to remain as cold and uninvolved as she is. Holden becomes interested in her as a person, asking her name and noticing her youth. His attempts to engage her in conversation fail, but he finds himself feeling sorry for her. When he hangs up her dress, he imagines her buying it in a store and the salesman thinking she was 'a regular girl', and this makes Holden 'feel sad as hell' (p. 100).

The episode reveals much about Holden's attitudes to relationships. It confirms his sensitivity towards others and demonstrates that while

cut.

he wishes to lose his virginity, a sexual relationship in which there is no affection or respect is impossible for him. For Holden it represents another disillusioning encounter with the adult world, offering him further evidence that the society of his elders is sordid and corrupt.

CHAPTER 14, *pp. 104–10*

Holden is feeling very dejected and talks out loud to his dead brother, Allie, something he occasionally does when he is miserable. He relates how he once refused to let Allie join him and a friend on a shooting trip. When he imagines he is talking to Allie, he tells him that he may come and arranges to meet him. After his distressing experience with the prostitute, Holden finds comfort in memories of Allie and their shared childhood and seeks in his imagination to rectify an action in the past that he now regrets.

Holden next gives his views on religion. He says he is 'sort of an atheist' (p. 104), but it is clear that he admires Jesus, whose spirit of forgiveness impresses him. He recalls arguing with a Quaker boy over whether Judas went to Hell after he committed suicide: 'I said I'd bet a thousand bucks that Jesus never sent old Judas to Hell' (p. 105). He dislikes the formality and insincerity of organized religion and criticizes the 'Holy Joe voices' adopted by ministers when they deliver sermons, saying, 'I don't see why the hell they can't talk in their natural voice. They sound so phoney when they talk' (p. 105).

Sunny returns to Holden's room, accompanied by the liftman, Maurice, and they demand another five dollars from him. Maurice had told Holden a prostitute would cost him five dollars (which Holden has paid), yet he now claims he said the price was ten dollars. When Holden refuses to pay any more, Sunny takes the money from his wallet. Holden protests loudly and, in spite of the fact he is crying, begins insulting Maurice, who responds by hitting him. After Holden has fallen to the floor, Sunny and Maurice leave. Holden is, as Maurice recognizes, a 'high-class kid' (p. 107), who has in many respects led a sheltered, privileged existence. In his dealings with Maurice and the prostitute he has come across a very different kind of life – one that is brutal, sordid and dishonest. Although he has no chance of preventing Sunny and Maurice from stealing his money, Holden does not give in meekly and he offers strong verbal resistance. In the previous chapter he claimed he was 'yellow', but he is clearly not a physical coward.

As elsewhere in the novel, Holden escapes the grimness of reality by exercising his imagination. He pretends that Maurice has shot him in the stomach and pictures himself staggering downstairs with a revolver, killing Maurice and then returning to his room, where Jane bandages his wound.

CHAPTER 15, *pp. 111–19*

Holden sleeps for a few hours and when he wakes up, he decides to telephone Sally Hayes. He does not really like Sally, but she is good-looking and he is feeling very lonely. He considers her 'quite a little phoney' (p. 111). Evidence of this is the way in which she acts as if she does not know it is Holden on the telephone and her affected use of the word 'grand' when Holden proposes going to a matinée theatre performance. Nor is Holden convinced when she claims that two young men, both from prestigious educational establishments – Harvard University and the Military Academy at West Point – are frantically pursuing her.

Holden checks out of his hotel and in the taxi to Grand Central Station he counts his money. He does not have much left and admits he is 'a goddam spendthrift at heart' (p. 113). As well as spending freely, he often forgets to pick up change in clubs and restaurants. This carelessness with money may partly be the result of his wealthy background (he has never been financially deprived), but it also reflects Holden's rejection of materialistic values. That he has an intense dislike of those who judge others according to their wealth and social status has already been made clear, and it is therefore unsurprising that he should consider money unimportant. He has a similar attitude towards possessions: in Chapter 13 he revealed, 'One of my troubles is, I never care too much when I lose something . . . I never seem to have anything that if I lost it I'd care too much' (p. 94). Further light is shed on this aspect of Holden's character when he recalls falling out with Dick Slagle, a boy with whom he shared a room at Elkton Hills School, because they had different kinds of suitcases (p. 114). While Slagle's suitcases looked very inexpensive, Holden's were made of genuine leather; it became clear that Slagle was embarrassed by his bags and resented Holden's affluence (he kept calling Holden's possessions '*bourgeois*'). After two months both boys asked to be moved to different rooms. It distresses Holden that material differences should cause such bad feeling: 'You think if they're intelligent and all, the other person, and have a good sense of humour, that they don't give a damn whose suitcases are better, but they do' (p. 115).

As Holden reflects on his attitude to money, he also imparts a little more information about his parents (p. 113). His father is a successful corporation lawyer who likes to invest money in Broadway shows. His mother's nerves were shaken by Allie's death, and since it occurred she 'hasn't felt too healthy' (p. 113). Holden is worried about the effect his latest expulsion will have upon her.

At the railway station Holden goes into a sandwich bar for breakfast and he is joined at his table by two nuns. He gives them ten dollars for their charity collection and when they leave, he tries to persuade them to allow him to pay their bill. Holden behaves with characteristic generosity here and his lack of financial greed is again highlighted. The nuns are schoolteachers, and Holden discusses with them the books he has studied in his English classes. Holden likes the nuns and 'enjoyed talking to them a lot' (p. 117). They are gentle (one has 'a helluva kind face'), unpretentious and virtuous, and as such represent a marked contrast to the brutality, insincerity and dishonesty Holden has recently encountered. Because they are nuns they are set apart from the rest of adult society and are untainted by its corruption; Holden is once more drawn to those who are pure and innocent. Part of their purity is their rejection of sex, and this helps to explain why Holden is so relaxed with them. He feels more secure in the company of women (or girls) when there is no possibility of sexual involvement. In this respect they are similar to Ernest Morrow's mother (Chapter 8), and it is appropriate that one of the nuns should remind Holden of her (p. 117).

CHAPTER 16, *pp. 120–28*

Holden compares other women he knows, such as his aunt and Sally Hayes's mother, with the nuns he has just met. He likes the nuns because they are not materialistic and he admires their selflessness and their lack of social vanity. Although his aunt helps charitable causes, Holden cannot imagine she would do so if she had to dress as simply as the nuns: 'when she does anything charitable she's always very well dressed and has lipstick on and all that crap' (p. 120). He is sure that if Sally Hayes's mother were collecting for charity and nobody spoke to her, 'she'd hand in her basket and then go some place swanky for lunch' (p. 120).

Before meeting Sally Hayes, Holden walks to Broadway to buy a record for Phoebe. On the way he passes a married couple and their young son, who have just been to church. The family is poor, but the boy seems happy as he walks along the road, oblivious of the traffic and his parents. Holden says the boy was singing the song 'If a body catch a body coming through the rye'. This is the first reference in the book to the novel's title, though the lyrics' significance will not be explained until Chapter 22. The song was written in the eighteenth century by Robert Burns and, as Phoebe later tells him, Holden is in fact mistaken about the words, which should be 'If a body *meet* a body coming through the rye' (p. 179). Holden's response when he hears the boy singing illustrates again how he is drawn to the innocence of childhood: 'It made me feel better. It made me feel not so depressed any more' (p. 122).

Holden's purchase of a pair of theatre tickets for the play *I Know My Love* leads him into a short discourse on acting. He dislikes acting because it usually appears forced and unnatural, and this provides further evidence of how much he values honesty and sincerity: 'I hate actors. They never act like people' (p. 123). He prefers to read a play, because when 'an actor acts it out, I hardly listen. I keep worrying about whether he's going to do something phoney every minute' (p. 124). Even with good actors the performance is marred by the actor's self-consciousness: 'And if any actor's really good, you can always tell he *knows* he's good, and that spoils it' (p. 123).

Holden goes to look for Phoebe in the park where she often goes roller-skating on Sundays. Phoebe is not there, but Holden sees a girl of about her age and asks her if she knows his sister. After speaking to the girl, Holden helps her to tighten her skate. Holden's fondness for children is again demonstrated. He describes her as a 'nice, polite little kid' (p. 125) and says that most children behave like that when you are kind to them.

Holden walks through the park to the Museum of Natural History, a place his schoolteacher would often take his class to when Holden was about Phoebe's age. Holden remembers his childhood visits to the museum with pleasure: 'I get very happy when I think about it' (p. 126). Significantly, what Holden liked most about the museum was that 'everything always stayed right where it was' (p. 127). This reflects Holden's attitude to the changes in human nature that occur with the passing of time. The way in which the innocence of childhood is gradually eroded distresses him, and he wishes that it could somehow be preserved: 'Certain things they should stay the way they are. You ought to be able to stick them in one of those big glass cases and just leave them alone' (p. 128). When he visited the museum as a child, he was aware that while it remained the same, he was changing, and he realizes that Phoebe, who now visits the museum as he used to, is changing in the same way. This saddens him: 'I thought how she'd see the same stuff I used to see, and how *she*'d be different every time she saw it. It didn't exactly depress me to think about it, but it didn't make me feel gay as hell, either' (p. 128).

When he reaches the museum, however, Holden has no desire to go inside. This takes him by surprise, as it does the reader. He is, perhaps, unconsciously recognizing and accepting that time *has* passed; he has grown older and cannot hope to re-enter the world of his childhood.

CHAPTER 17, *pp. 129–40*

Holden meets Sally Hayes at the Biltmore Hotel. Although he finds her extremely good-looking and felt like marrying her the moment he saw her coming up the stairs, he admits, 'I didn't even *like* her much' (p. 130). He is embarrassed by her loud voice and affected manner.

The play they see follows a married couple through the course of their lives. Holden cannot get involved in the story as the characters are 'all just a bunch of actors' (p. 131). The leading actors play their parts well, but Holden believes that their performances, like Ernie's at the club, suffer because they clearly know that they are good and are guilty of 'showing off' (p. 132).

During the interval the foyer is crowded with 'phonies' – members of the audience who are loudly expressing their opinions of the play so that others will be impressed by their intelligence and taste. Holden singles out for special criticism the false nonchalance of a film actor who is trying to pretend he is not aware that people are looking at him. Sally meets George, an acquaintance of hers who attends Andover College. He is another phoney, and Holden finds their warm greeting of each other 'nauseating' (p. 133). George has a 'snobby' voice and uses pretentious language, calling the leading actors in the play 'angels' (p. 133).

After the play Sally suggests they go ice-skating, because, according to Holden, she wants to be admired wearing a short skating skirt. They have drinks at the ice-rink and as they talk, all Holden's accumulated rage and despair is suddenly released in a savage tirade against conventional society. Holden's speech is confused and uncontrolled, but this is one of the most important episodes in the novel and is central to an understanding of his character. He begins by attacking the aggression, artificiality and pretentiousness of urban life. He cites the worship of the motor car as symptomatic of a society that is devoid of feeling. He then denounces schools, which inculcate the materialistic values of the adult world: 'all you do is study, so that you can learn enough to be smart enough to be able to buy a goddam Cadillac some day' (p. 137). He condemns the unhealthy, claustrophobic atmosphere of boys' schools, where 'all you do is talk about girls and liquor and sex all day' (p. 137). Holden desperately wishes to escape from the narrowness and inhumanity of modern civilization and he asks Sally to run away with him. He wants to live a simple, natural life in a rural environment, away from the pressures of city life: 'We'll stay in these cabin camps and stuff like that till the dough runs out. Then, when the dough runs out, I could get a job somewhere and we could live somewhere with a brook and all, and, later on, we could get married or something. I could chop all our own wood in the winter-time and all' (p. 138).

Sally's reaction to Holden's outburst is a mixture of irritation and incomprehension. She asks him to stop shouting and it is clear that she wants him to change the subject. At one point she admits, 'I don't know what you're even talking about' (p. 136). Her lack of sympathy and understanding arises from the fact that she is content with society as it is. She accepts the values of an adult, urban world and expects that her life will follow a conventional pattern. When Holden proposes running away, she tells him, 'We'll have oodles of time to do those things – all those things. I mean after you go to college and all, and if we should get married and all' (p. 138). Holden states that by the end of the conversation, 'We both hated each other's guts' (p. 139). In his anger and frustration he swears at Sally and then regrets having done so. Looking back at the episode, he recognizes their essential incompatibility and realizes that asking her to leave New York with him was a mistake: 'She wouldn't have been anybody to go with' (p. 140).

CHAPTER 18, *pp. 141–7*

After he leaves the ice-rink, Holden tries to telephone Jane Gallagher, but there is no reply. Earlier in the day he had rung her home and put the receiver down when her mother answered (p. 122). Holden's attempts to communicate with others seem, for one reason or another, to be doomed to failure. He then calls Carl Luce, who had been a fellow pupil at Whooton School. Although Holden admits that he does not like Luce much, he respects his intelligence and feels in need of company. They arrange to have a drink together later that evening.

Before meeting Luce, Holden goes to see a film. The film is preceded by a stage show that includes a celebration of Christmas with actors dressed as angels and carrying crucifixes. Holden claims to be an atheist, but he has some regard for religion and is disgusted by the insincerity of the performance. He says of the actors, 'you could tell they could hardly wait to get a cigarette or something' (p. 143). The film itself confirms Holden's low opinion of cinema, for it has an implausible, nauseatingly sentimental storyline. Holden finds himself compelled to watch out of astonishment at its sheer awfulness: 'It was so putrid I couldn't take my eyes off it' (p. 144).

The film told the story of a man who lost his memory after fighting in the Second World War, which causes Holden to think about war as he walks over to the Wicker Bar to meet Carl Luce. He says he would hate to have to join the army, not because he is a pacifist but because he could not stand being forced into the company of people he did not like. Holden's attitude to the army reflects his nonconformist outlook; he values his independence and cannot identify with institutions. He had joined the Boy Scouts once but had left after a week.

CHAPTER 19, *pp. 148–55*

The Wicker Bar is a fashionable night-spot where 'the phonies are coming in the window' (p. 148). The bartender is snobbish and insincere, ignoring customers who are not wealthy or famous and speaking ingratiatingly to those who are.

Carl Luce is arrogant and affected and strives to appear a sophisticated man of the world. The Wicker Bar, which he had chosen as a meeting-place, is a suitable environment for him. He tells Holden that his girlfriend is a Chinese sculptress in her late thirties who lives in Greenwich Village, the artists' quarter of New York. Asked whether he likes the fact that his girlfriend is Chinese, he replies with characteristic pretentiousness, 'I simply happen to find Eastern philosophy more satisfactory than Western' (p. 152). His manner towards Holden is aloof and disdainful. As soon as he arrives, he tells Holden he can stay only for a few minutes. He deliberately gives Holden the impression that he is bored by him and makes it plain that he considers him immature. He is completely unsympathetic when Holden tells him of his loneliness: as he is about to go, Holden pleads, 'Have just one more drink . . . Please. I'm lonesome as hell. No kidding' (p. 155), but Luce leaves anyway.

Holden is aware that Luce is phoney and unfriendly, but he is impressed by his intellect and by his knowledge and experience of sex. Holden's own feelings about sex are confused, and he hopes

Luce will be able to resolve some of his difficulties. As he questions Luce, it is again made clear that for Holden a sexual relationship can only exist if there is also a spiritual empathy. But he doubts the wisdom of this attitude. He is probably thinking of his recent experience with the prostitute when he tells Luce, 'You know what the trouble with me is? I can never get really sexy – I mean *really* sexy – with a girl I don't like a lot. I mean I have to *like* her a lot. If I don't, I sort of lose my goddam desire for her and all. Boy, it really screws up my sex life something awful. My sex life stinks' (p. 153). Luce predictably has little sympathy for Holden's plight and does not give him the guidance he is seeking. He suggests, however, that Holden should see a psychoanalyst – a prophetic indication of where Holden's confusion and despair will eventually lead him.

CHAPTER 20, *pp. 156–63*

This chapter emphasizes Holden's isolation. Before leaving the bar, he makes a number of attempts to communicate with others, all of which end in failure. First he asks the waiter to invite the club's singer, Valencia, to join him for a drink. Nothing comes of this and he suspects the waiter probably did not even pass his message on. Next he makes a drunken phone-call to Sally Hayes. When he says he still intends to come to see her on Christmas Eve, she agrees, but Holden becomes increasingly incoherent and she hangs up on him. In the men's room Holden tries to strike up a conversation with the club's piano player. He asks him to speak to Valencia for him and praises his playing. The pianist advises Holden to go home and walks out while Holden is still trying to talk to him. As Holden is leaving, his loneliness and depression are such that he starts to cry. Finally, when Holden collects his coat, he tries to make a date with the cloakroom girl. She is friendly, but insists that Holden should go home and go to bed.

Holden walks to Central Park to see whether any ducks are at the lake. Here the bleakness and desolation of the setting highlight Holden's solitude and hopelessness: 'I kept walking and walking, and it kept getting darker and darker and spookier and spookier. I didn't see one person the whole time I was in the park' (p. 160). Holden is on the point of spiritual collapse, and this is reflected in what happens to Phoebe's record: he accidentally drops it and it 'broke into about fifty pieces' (p. 160). His mental and emotional despondency is accompanied by physical distress. He is shivering, and his hair, which he had plunged into a sink full of cold water at the nightclub, is filled with pieces of ice. He wonders if he is going to die of pneumonia and then begins to consider death. He would not like to be buried in a cemetery, 'surrounded by dead guys' (p. 161). He recalls visiting Allie's grave with his parents when it was raining. He and the other visitors were able to escape, but Allie was not, and Holden finds the thought of Allie's body in his grave with the rain pouring down on it almost unbearable. He no longer goes to the cemetery.

Holden counts the loose change in his pocket and then skims the coins across the surface of the lake. This may be seen as a symbolic renunciation of materialistic values. Money matters little to Holden, and he has contempt for those who judge others according to their wealth and social status. At this point in the novel Holden's alienation from others and from the attitudes and values of contemporary society seems total, but there is one person with whom he still wishes to communicate and with whom he is able to make contact – his sister, Phoebe. He knows that his death would greatly upset her and decides that if he is going to die of pneumonia, he must speak to her first.

CHAPTER 21, *pp. 164–72*

Holden lets himself into his family's apartment and steals into D.B.'s room, where Phoebe is sleeping. In the presence of his sister he no longer feels lonely and unhappy: 'I felt swell, for a change' (p. 166). As he watches Phoebe while she sleeps, the strength of his affection for her, and for children in general, is clear: 'She was laying there asleep, with her face sort of on the side of the pillow. She had her mouth way open. It's funny. You take adults, they look lousy when they're asleep and they have their mouths way open, but kids don't. Kids look all right' (p. 166). He takes a close interest in Phoebe's activities and habits and describes with pride the way she dresses

('Phoebe always has some dress on that can kill you', p. 166) and the neatness with which she has arranged her clothes by the bed. He finds many of her attitudes and actions endearing: her fondness for D.B.'s room because it is the biggest in the apartment and has a large desk ('You can hardly see her when she's doing her homework', p. 166), her invention of new middle names for herself and her huge number of notebooks. Holden reads through one of these books, and his love of children is again apparent when he comments, 'I can read that kind of stuff, some kid's notebook, Phoebe's or anybody, all day and all night long' (p. 168).

Phoebe's reaction when Holden wakes her shows that her feelings for him are equally strong. She puts her arms around his neck and, says Holden, was 'glad as hell to see me' (p. 168). When Holden tells her he has broken the record he bought for her, she takes the pieces from him and says she is going to save them. She is a lively child and talks excitedly about her part in a school play and the film she saw that afternoon. Since leaving Pencey Prep Holden has suffered a series of rejections and disillusioning experiences, but he is now in the company of an innocent, guileless child who responds to his presence with warmth and enthusiasm. He begins to relax and stops worrying over whether his parents (who are out at a party) will catch him at home. Phoebe becomes upset, however, when she realizes that Holden has been expelled from school and, after punching her brother on the leg, she covers her face with a pillow.

CHAPTER 22, *pp. 173–80*

When Phoebe asks Holden why he was expelled, he explains at length his dislike of Pencey Prep. Unlike most of the other people he has encountered, Phoebe is somebody in whom he can confide, who is interested in what he has to say and who understands him: 'She always listens when you tell her something. And the funny part is she knows, half the time, what the hell you're talking about. She really does' (p. 174). He tells Phoebe about the phoniness of the school and the cruelty shown to boys such as Ackley. Even Mr Spencer, a teacher Holden liked, could be obsequious and insincere, laughing to flatter the headmaster when he cracked a joke.

Phoebe realizes that Holden's disenchantment extends beyond Pencey Prep and tells him, 'You don't like *anything* that's happening' (p. 176). Holden protests, but when Phoebe challenges him to name one thing he likes, he struggles for a reply. He thinks of the nuns he met at breakfast (Chapter 15) and of James Castle, a pupil at Elkton Hills who had been told by a group of school bullies to take back something he had said. He refused and remained defiant even when the bullies began assaulting him. Finally, rather than give in, he jumped out of the window and fell to his death. Holden clearly admired his courage and integrity. His sympathy for the boy demonstrates again his compassion for those who are vulnerable and defenceless: James Castle was 'very quiet' and 'a skinny little weak-looking guy' (p. 177). Holden does not mention the nuns and James Castle to Phoebe, but he does tell her that he likes Allie, and sitting and talking to her. Phoebe is unimpressed: Allie does not count because he is dead and talking to her 'isn't anything *really*' (p. 178). Phoebe's response is interesting and draws attention to the extent of Holden's dissatisfaction with life, suggesting that it may be excessive. Holden feels the strongest affection for children (Phoebe), those who are dead (Allie and James Castle) and those who are outside society (the nuns). The adult world in general he finds unworthy of his respect and his love.

This is confirmed when Phoebe asks Holden what he would like to be. A conventional adult career – becoming a lawyer like his father, for instance – does not appeal to him because it brings material rewards but no spiritual fulfilment: 'All you do is make a lot of dough and play golf and play bridge and buy cars and drink martinis and look like a hot-shot' (p. 179). When Holden tells Phoebe what he would really like to be, the significance of the novel's title is at last explained. He refers to the song he heard the little boy singing that morning, 'If a body catch a body comin' through the rye', and says he would like to be 'the catcher in the rye' (pp. 179–80). He imagines thousands of children playing in a field of rye that is perched on a cliff and pictures himself standing on the edge catching the children who run too close to it. Holden thus sees himself as a guardian of the innocent. His fantasy is appropriate because, as the novel has already shown, he has a protective attitude towards those who are vulnerable (especially children) and wishes he could preserve the innocence of childhood. Nevertheless it is a fantasy: children cannot be prevented from entering the corrupt world of their elders.

This chapter has implied more criticism of Holden's attitudes than any previous one, suggesting that they are negative and unrealistic. It has also emphasized by contrast Phoebe's remarkable maturity and insight. There is much truth in her observation that Holden does not like '*anything* that's happening', and she shows that she is more practical than her brother when he says he may go and work on a ranch in Colorado and she replies, 'Don't make me laugh. You can't even ride a horse' (p. 173). Holden's point of view has inevitably dominated the novel and until now there has been little to set against it. Phoebe, however, encourages the reader to examine Holden more objectively.

CHAPTER 23, *pp. 181–7*

Holden telephones his former English teacher at Elkton Hills, Mr Antolini, and arranges to call on him. He says Mr Antolini was 'about the best teacher I ever had' (p. 181). He had a sense of humour and would laugh and joke with his pupils, but they never lost their respect for him. Holden admired his behaviour when James Castle committed suicide: he put his coat over the boy's body, even though it became bloodstained, and carried him to the infirmary. It is already clear that Mr Antolini, who will appear in the next chapter, is an important character, for he is one of the very few adults who is liked and trusted by Holden.

Holden hides in a cupboard when his parents return. His mother comes into the bedroom and speaks to Phoebe. This is the only time either of his parents appears in the novel. She is affectionate towards Phoebe, but it is possible to sense that she has been an unhappy woman since Allie's death: Holden can tell that she had not enjoyed herself at the party and when she complains of a headache, he observes that this is a frequent occurrence.

After his mother has left the room, Holden asks Phoebe if he may borrow some money. Phoebe insists on his taking the money she has saved for Christmas. Holden is so moved by his sister's generosity that he begins to cry, and his tears are a sign of his underlying despair. Phoebe again shows her concern for her brother when she tries to comfort him.

CHAPTER 24, *pp. 188–200*

Holden has kept in close contact with Mr Antolini since leaving Elkton Hills. He has been to his apartment several times and Mr Antolini in turn has frequently been invited to the Caulfields' for dinner. He has become a family friend and had advised D.B. against going to Hollywood; he tells Holden he had lunch with his father two weeks previously. Mr Antolini's manner is relaxed and friendly, and he appears not to mind being disturbed by Holden at such a late hour. Holden is impressed by his intelligence and his sharp sense of humour, though he dislikes the element of pretentiousness and pomposity in his speech ('You and Pencey are no longer one', p. 189). He is married to a rich, older woman, who makes only a fleeting appearance; like her husband, she makes Holden welcome, and she prepares a tray of coffee and cakes before returning to bed.

Holden talks to Mr Antolini about Pencey Prep and tells him that he failed a course called Oral Expression. Each boy had to give talks to the rest of the class and if he strayed from his chosen subject, the other pupils were meant to shout, 'Digression!' at him. Holden says his problem was that he *likes* digressions. He enjoys listening to people talk about things that genuinely interest them and does not mind if they do not stick rigidly to one topic. Holden's attitude towards digressions is clearly reflected in his own narrative technique: in telling the reader of his experiences around the time he left Pencey Prep he has frequently given detailed accounts of incidents that occurred further back in time and has interrupted his narrative to give his opinion on a variety of issues.

Mr Antolini tries to discuss with Holden his attitude to life in general and shows considerable insight into Holden's present state of mind. He can see that Holden is deeply troubled and believes he may be heading for 'some kind of a terrible, terrible fall' (p. 193). He knows that Holden finds the world a disappointing place and says there have been people like him before, people who 'were looking for something their own environment couldn't supply them with' (p. 194). He fears that Holden's discontent will eventually become absolute and he will give up looking and surrender to despair. Mr Antolini tells him he urgently needs to find a way out of his melancholy and says that education, which Holden has rejected, can help him to do this. Through the study of history and literature he will discover that he is 'not the first person who was ever confused and frightened and even sickened by human behaviour' (p. 196). Studying the thoughts and experiences of others will stimulate him and help him come to terms with himself.

Mr Antolini's advice is intelligent, sympathetic and constructive, but Holden is in an unreceptive mood. He feels ill and exhausted and cannot prevent himself from yawning, though he knows he is being rude. Mr Antolini remains good-humoured and tells Holden it is time they made up a bed for him. Holden falls asleep on the couch and is suddenly wakened by something touching his head. When he realizes that Mr Antolini is stroking him, he jumps to his feet and, despite Mr Antolini's protests, hurriedly makes his excuses and leaves the apartment. This episode inevitably reinforces Holden's belief that the adult world is sordid and corrupt. The experience is all the more disillusioning because Mr Antolini is somebody Holden had admired and trusted. The episode also shows again that Holden is frightened and confused by sex; his reaction to Mr Antolini's apparent homosexuality is a mixture of terror and revulsion.

CHAPTER 25, *pp. 201–19*

Holden has been badly shaken by his experience at Mr Antolini's apartment and passes an uncomfortable few hours at Grand Central Station. After he has left the station, he has a strange sensation as he walks along Fifth Avenue: every time he has to cross a road he feels that he is going to vanish before he reaches the other side. It is as if Holden's sense of alienation from the world around him is so acute that he believes he is actually about to disappear from it. As at the beginning of Chapter 14, his thoughts turn in his distress to Allie. At the end of every block he asks his brother to help him cross the road.

Holden decides he will leave New York and hitch-hike to the West. His plan is similar to the suggestion he made to Sally Hayes in Chapter 17: he intends earning enough money to build himself a cabin in the woods, where he will continue to live for the rest of his life. Holden's scheme indicates that he would like to escape from civilization, which he has found to be brutal, hypocritical and corrupt, and that he no longer wishes to communicate with others. He would pretend to be a deaf mute and then 'I'd be through with having conversations for the rest of my life' (p. 205). If he wanted to get married, he would find another deaf mute; if they had children, 'we'd hide them somewhere' (p. 206), ensuring their innocence was not tainted by contact with society. The pretentiousness and in-sincerity that Holden despises would be firmly excluded. He would allow his family to visit him, but 'I'd have this rule that nobody could do anything phoney when they visited me. If anybody tried to do anything phoney, they couldn't stay' (p. 211).

He wants to say goodbye to Phoebe before he leaves and goes to her school, where he hands in a note asking his sister to meet him at lunchtime. At the school he comes across a swear-word written on a wall. Holden is shocked, upset and angry: 'I kept wanting to kill whoever'd written it' (p. 207). He imagines it was written on the wall by an adult who had slipped into the building late at night, and he is dis-tressed to think of the damaging effect it might have on the children in the school. Fulfilling his role as the catcher in the rye, the protector of children's innocence, Holden rubs the graffiti from the wall. As he leaves the building, however, he finds a similar inscription on another wall. This has been scratched on and cannot be removed. Holden reflects, 'It's hopeless, anyway. If you had a million years to do it in, you couldn't rub out even *half* the "– you" signs in the world. It's impossible' (p. 208). This is an important passage, because it suggests that Holden is beginning to recognize that corruption is inevitable in life and cannot be avoided. There is more evidence of this when he finds yet another obscenity written on a wall of the museum where he has arranged to meet Phoebe and observes, 'You can't never find a place that's nice and peaceful, because there isn't any. You may *think* there is, but once you get there, when you're not looking, somebody'll sneak up and write "– you" right under your nose' (p. 210). Holden seems to be acknowledging that his dream of escaping to an idyllic life in the woods can never become a reality.

The conclusion of the chapter offers further confirmation that Holden is moving towards an acceptance of the world as it is. When Phoebe meets him, she is carrying a suitcase and asks if she may come with him, but Holden says no. He tells her that anyway he has changed his mind about leaving and is going home. Phoebe refuses to return to school, so he visits the zoo and the park with her. At the park she rides on a merry-go-round and, like the other children, keeps trying to reach the gold ring in the middle. Although Holden is afraid that Phoebe might fall, 'I didn't say anything or do anything. The thing with kids is, if they want to grab for the gold ring, you have to let them do it, and not say anything. If they fall off, they fall off, but it's bad if you say anything to them' (p. 218). This passage contrasts strikingly with Holden's earlier description of himself as the catcher in the rye, the protective figure who intervenes to prevent children from falling. It suggests that Holden now realizes that children cannot be shielded for ever from the hazards of adulthood; they must be allowed to grow, even if that growth results in the eventual and inevitable loss of their innocence.

Holden no longer wishes to retreat from the realities of life and intends to go home. His sister's love for him (she says she is not cross with him any more, kisses him and puts his red hunting hat on his head) and his love for her help reconcile him to the world. As he sits watching Phoebe on the roundabout, he is at peace with himself and with life; oblivious of the rain that begins falling, he is near to tears because he 'felt so damn happy' (p. 219).

CHAPTER 26, *p. 220*

In this short final chapter Holden returns to the present. After he went back home, the physical and mental stress he had experienced led to a breakdown in his health, and he is now in a hospital where he is undergoing psychoanalysis. Some readers have seen this ending as pessimistic in that Holden's spirit seems to have been broken by society and he is now a sad defeated figure. The previous chapter, however, suggested that Holden was moving towards a vision of the world that included an acceptance of its imperfections. Aware of the unpredictability of life, Holden admits that he does not know what the future holds, but he *thinks* he will begin his new school in September in a more positive spirit. Moreover, as the closing sentences reveal, in spite of all he has endured, his love for others is undiminished: 'About all I know is, I sort of *miss* everybody I told about. Even old Stradlater and Ackley, for instance. I think I even miss that goddam Maurice' (p. 220).

Characters

HOLDEN CAULFIELD

The Catcher in the Rye describes an adolescent's struggle to come to terms with the adult world he is about to enter. Holden Caulfield is a decent, principled young man, but the society of his elders consistently disappoints him: he is repelled by its materialism, its hypocrisy and its cruelty.

The early chapters of the novel reveal that Holden has a sensitive, compassionate nature. Before leaving Pencey Prep, for example, he makes a point of calling on Mr Spencer, the elderly teacher who has shown him kindness in the past. He feels sorry for Selma Thurmer, the headmaster's daughter, and for Robert Ackley, a boy who is generally shunned by his fellow pupils. When he goes into Agerstown on Saturday evening with Mal Brossard, he invites Ackley to join them. Holden's account of his life at Pencey also emphasizes his own isolation, however. He has no close friends at Pencey and feels no loyalty towards the school. At the annual football match against Saxon Hall he does not watch with the other students; instead he looks down on the game from a nearby hill and leaves before it is over. When the novel opens, he is about to be expelled from Pencey and the reader learns that he has experienced similar problems at other schools. As he later tries to explain to Sally Hayes, he finds it impossible to identify with an educational system that promotes materialism and social conformity: 'all you do is study, so that you can learn enough to be smart enough to be able to buy a goddam Cadillac some day' (p. 137).

Holden's experiences in New York after he leaves Pencey indicate that he feels alienated not only from his school but from society as a whole. His beliefs and values repeatedly conflict with those of the people around him. Insincerity, or 'phoniness', fills him with contempt, and he finds it pervades the adult world. He observes it in the affected behaviour of the crowd at Ernie's nightclub and in the pretentious conversation of the audience at the theatre he goes to with Sally Hayes. Sally herself was 'quite a little phoney' (p. 111) and Holden is embarrassed by her forced enthusiasm and extravagant manner. Although he is from an affluent background, Holden himself is not materialistic and is careless with money and possessions. People he encounters, however, continually judge others according to their wealth and social status. Ernie is a social snob who 'won't hardly even talk to you unless you're a big shot or a celebrity' (p. 85) and the bartender at the Wicker Bar similarly ignores customers who are not rich or famous. Faith Cavendish, the girl whose telephone number Holden was given by a young man at a party, suddenly becomes friendly when he implies that he is a student at Princeton University. The three girls from out of town whom he meets at the Edmont Hotel seem to be interested only in spotting film stars.

Holden admits that his thoughts on sex are confused, but here again adults do not set him the kind of example he would wish to follow. The Edmont Hotel was 'full of perverts' (p. 65) and, soon after arriving there, he watches from his window the degenerate behaviour of some of the other guests. He is offered the services of a prostitute and is upset by the girl's cold, unemotional manner. Unable to share her detached attitude, he cannot bring himself to go to bed with her. Later Mr Antolini, a former teacher and, ironically, one of the few adults liked and respected by Holden, disgusts him by making what appear to be homosexual advances.

Despite these discouraging experiences, Holden repeatedly tries to communicate with others, inviting taxi drivers to join him for drinks, speaking to strangers on trains and in bars and nightclubs and arranging to meet people he does not really like (such as Sally Hayes and Carl Luce). He frequently describes himself as 'lonesome' and is clearly in desperate need of understanding and love. Almost all his attempts to establish contact fail, however, either because his offers of friendship are rejected or because he finds he is with someone he does not respect or who does not comprehend him.

It is noticeable that those whom Holden finds he is most able to admire are set outside conventional adult society. He likes the two nuns, who have rejected materialism and are morally pure. Others held in high regard by Holden are no longer part of the world simply because they are dead. He admired the integrity of James Castle, who committed suicide rather than give in to school bullies. Allie, his younger brother who died of leukaemia at the age of eleven, is recalled almost with reverence. Holden's tenderness towards him also illustrates his love of children, who are free from the corruption of adulthood. He talks to children at the park and in the museum and when he sees a little boy singing in the street, he says, 'It made me feel better. It made me feel not so depressed any more' (p. 122). Jane Gallagher, with whom he had enjoyed an innocent love relationship two summers previously, he still thinks of as a child. He has more of a rapport with his younger sister, Phoebe, than with any adult: 'if you tell old Phoebe something, she knows exactly what the hell you're talking about' (p. 72).

Holden's regard for the virtuousness of children and corresponding distaste for adult life account for his wish to be the catcher in the rye, the protector of childhood innocence. We see him attempting to fulfil this role when he attacks Ward Stradlater, who appeared to threaten Jane Gallagher's innocence, and when he rubs out the swearword written on the wall at Phoebe's school. He wishes children could remain uncorrupted. He likes the museum because the exhibits in it never change, and he reflects, 'Certain things they should stay the way they are. You ought to be able to stick them in one of those big glass cases and just leave them alone' (p. 128).

Some critics of the novel have felt that Holden's rejection of the adult world is too absolute and that J. D. Salinger identifies with it too closely. The hypocrisy and corruption Holden encounters in adult society are perhaps too pervasive to be credible. However, while the reader is encouraged to share Holden's pessimistic conclusions about human nature for much of the novel, alternative viewpoints emerge in the later chapters. Phoebe is distressed by Holden's despairing attitude and tells him, 'You don't like *anything* that's happening' (p. 176). Mr Antolini informs Holden that he is by no means the first person to have found human behaviour hard to accept and suggests that studying the experiences of others will help him to approach life more positively. Moreover, the concluding pages of the novel present a shift in Holden's own view of the world. His response to the obscene graffiti on the wall of the museum – 'You can't never find a place that's nice and peaceful, because there isn't any' (p. 210) – suggests a realization that corruption is an inevitable part of life, while his willingness to allow Phoebe to reach for the gold ring, and so risk falling, implies that he no longer sees himself as the catcher in the rye but accepts that children must lose their innocence and face the hazards of adulthood. The novel ends on a note of qualified hope: coming to terms with the world requires an acceptance of its imperfections, and Holden seems to have achieved this.

PHOEBE CAULFIELD

Of all the characters in the novel, Phoebe comes closest to satisfying Holden's need for understanding and love. It is significant that she is a child, and therefore untouched by the malevolence of the adult world.

Holden describes his ten-year-old sister with pride and affection. She is pretty and intelligent, and Holden admires the way she dresses and her skill at dancing. He is amused by her childish habits, such as the notebooks she keeps and the stories she writes about a girl detective whose name she misspells as 'Hazle Weatherfield'. He communicates more successfully with her than he does with adults or people of his own age: 'She always listens when you tell her something. And the funny part is she knows, half the time, what the hell you're talking about. She really does' (p. 174). He values her innocence and is saddened to think that as she grows older it will fade: at the museum he says, 'I thought how she'd see the same stuff I used to see, and how *she*'d be different every time she saw it' (p. 128).

When Holden is at his point of greatest despair, wandering lost and alone through the wintry desolation of Central Park, it is Phoebe he decides he must see. Watching her asleep in D.B.'s bed, he is lifted out of his depression: 'I felt swell, for a change' (p. 166). When she wakes up, Holden says she is 'glad as hell to see me' (p. 168). She throws her arms around his neck and tells him excitedly about the school play she is to appear in.

Phoebe obviously feels a deep affection for Holden, yet her attitude towards him is not wholly uncritical. She is angry and upset when she discovers that he has been expelled from yet another school and shows her disapproval by turning her back on him and burying her face in a pillow. Although her actions, as in this instance, are often endearingly childish, she shows intelligence and maturity when she tells Holden, 'You don't like *anything* that's happening' (p. 176). She recognizes the extent of his unhappiness, and her view that Holden's attitude to life is excessively pessimistic may be shared by the reader.

Phoebe plays an important part in helping Holden overcome his inability to accept the world as it is. At the museum he wishes that time could stand still, and later he tells Phoebe that he would like to be the catcher in the rye, a guardian of childhood innocence. But as he watches Phoebe trying to reach for the gold ring on the roundabout, he decides to leave her alone and allow her to risk falling; children must be allowed to grow and cannot be protected for ever from the realities of adult life. As he sits on the park bench, he is at last happy and at peace with the world; his love of Phoebe and the knowledge of her love for him fill him with joy: 'I felt so damn happy all of a sudden, the way old Phoebe kept going round and round. I was damn near bawling, I felt so damn happy' (p. 219).

ALLIE CAULFIELD

Holden's younger brother, Allie, died of leukaemia at the age of eleven. Holden was thirteen at the time and the loss of his brother is probably responsible for much of his loneliness and depression. Holden says Allie was good-natured and had a strong sense of humour; he was never angry at anyone and when something amused him, he would laugh so much that he nearly fell off his chair. He was also clever, and was the most intelligent member of the family, according to Holden. When Allie died, Holden showed his anger and despair by smashing the windows of the family garage with his fist. Allie is still frequently in Holden's thoughts. He has kept Allie's baseball glove, which Allie had covered with poems written in green ink, and describes it when Stradlater asks him to write a composition for him. Holden reveals that he often speaks aloud to Allie when he is feeling low. In his imagination he relives a shooting trip Allie had wanted to go on and tells him he may come after all. Towards the end of the novel Holden has the unnerving sensation as he is walking down the street that he is about to disappear; he looks to Allie for help and repeatedly says, 'Allie, don't let me disappear' (p. 204). When Phoebe, distressed by Holden's negative attitude to life, challenges him to name something he cares for, he says he likes Allie.

Allie is dead, but he is still of great importance to Holden. Like Phoebe, he is a symbol of childhood purity and innocence, a contrast to the hypocrisy and corruption of adult society. Although Allie's early death was a devastating blow, it means that Holden's conception of him need never alter; he is one child who is safe for ever from the corrupting influence of the adult world.

SALLY HAYES

Holden's friendship with Sally Hayes is symptomatic of his confusion over relationships with the opposite sex. He thinks she is very good-looking and asks her to run away with him, but says, 'I didn't even *like* her much' (p. 130). Their personalities are essentially incompatible.

Holden considers Sally is insincere and shallow, because she pretends not to know it is Holden on the telephone and uses affected words such as 'grand'. When they meet, her greeting of Holden is characteristically gushing: 'Holden! ... It's marvellous to see you! It's been *ages*' (p. 130). Holden is embarrassed by her loud, extrovert manner. At the theatre she is predictably enthusiastic about the Lunts, a fashionable acting couple, and annoys Holden by talking at length to a college student with a 'snobby' voice. They keep mentioning names as if to prove how many people they both know, and Holden describes it as 'the phoniest conversation you ever heard in your life' (p. 133).

Sally is present when all Holden's accumulated rage and dissatisfaction erupts in a lengthy, inarticulate attack on contemporary life. His remarks are addressed to her, but not because he believes she will be a sympathetic listener; the outburst has been coming for some time, and Sally just happens to be there when it occurs. He becomes so carried away, however, that he invites Sally to run away with him and set up home in a rural environment, away from the pressures and artificiality of urban life. Sally is bewildered by Holden's tirade and admits, 'I don't know what you're even talking about' (p. 136). She repeatedly asks him to stop shouting at her and Holden realizes that she is anxious for him to change the subject. Sally cannot identify with Holden's complaints, because she is thoroughly conventional in her attitudes and accepts the values of society unquestioningly. When Holden proposes escaping from New York, she says they will have time to travel together after Holden has been to college and if they subsequently marry. She responds to Holden's criticism of the schools he has been to by saying, 'Lots of boys get more out of school than *that*' (p. 137).

Holden states that by the end of the conversation they 'both hated each other's guts' (p. 139). His hostility towards her is such that he swears at her and she begins crying. He regrets being abusive to her but also realizes that they are fundamentally unsuited to each other. He knows asking her to run off with him was a mistake and reflects, 'I probably wouldn't've taken her even if she'd wanted to go with me. She wouldn't have been anybody to go with' (p. 140). The reader may find Holden rather harsh in his condemnation of Sally, but, in view of the differences in their attitudes and expectations, the conflict that arises between them is inevitable.

JANE GALLAGHER

Whereas his relationship with Sally Hayes is deeply and obviously flawed, Holden has happy memories of his friendship with Jane Gallagher. Two summers before the events described in the novel Jane's family lived next door to the Caulfields, and Holden spent much time in her company. As befitted their age, their relationship had been innocent and childlike. They played checkers, tennis and golf together and went to the cinema. Holden was physically attracted to Jane, but they 'never necked or horsed around much' (p. 84). He was content simply to hold hands with her: 'You never even worried, with Jane, whether your hand was sweaty or not. All you knew was, you were happy. You really were' (p. 84). Holden trusted Jane and felt close to her. She is the only person outside his family to whom he has shown Allie's baseball mitt and when he talked to her about Allie, she listened sympathetically.

Holden's friendship with Jane reveals much about his attitudes towards relationships. It shows that he most respects those in which there is affection and understanding as well as physical attraction. The fact that the relationship was spiritual rather than physical increases Holden's regard for it: he values the innocence of childhood and sees his friendship with Jane as pure and uncorrupted. It also illustrates Holden's sympathetic attitude towards those who are vulnerable and unhappy. Jane had a 'lousy childhood' (p. 36); her parents were divorced, and her mother's second husband, Mr Cudahy, was a drunken brute who would walk around naked in front of Jane. One day when Holden and Jane were on her front porch her stepfather came out and spoke to her; she ignored him, but after he had gone back into the house, she began to cry. Holden suspected Cudahy of having molested Jane, but she would not tell him what was wrong. Holden tried to comfort her, and it is clear that her distress still upsets him.

When Holden learns that Jane has a date with his room-mate, Ward Stradlater, he 'damn near dropped dead' (p. 35). After Stradlater has left to meet her, Holden cannot stop thinking about her. Essentially he is worried because he sees Stradlater, who is sexually experienced and untrustworthy with girls, as a threat to Jane's innocence: 'It made me so nervous I nearly went crazy. I already told you what a sexy bastard Stradlater was' (p. 38). When Stradlater returns, Holden is in a tense, hostile mood and finally, his voice shaking, he asks if Stradlater and Jane made love. Stradlater gives a light, non-committal reply and Holden launches a ferocious attack on him. Jane brings out in Holden his desire to be the catcher in the rye – the defender of childhood innocence.

In Holden's imagination Jane has become, like his dead brother, an idealized figure – a symbol of goodness and purity. Holden's vision of Allie can remain unchanged because he will never grow up, and his vision of Jane can remain unchanged because he has not seen her for almost two years and can continue to think of her as she was then. It does not occur to him that her character might have developed. It is appropriate that she never appears in the novel, for she represents something that is unattainable; Holden twice tries to telephone her, but he is unsuccessful on both occasions.

Mr ANTOLINI

Unlike the great majority of adult characters in the novel, Mr Antolini is liked and trusted by Holden. He taught Holden at Elkton Hills School and was 'about the best teacher I ever had' (p. 181). He was relaxed with his pupils and would allow them to joke with him, but always retained their respect. Holden particularly admired his behaviour when James Castle committed suicide: he covered the boy's bloodstained body with his own coat and carried him to the infirmary. Since Holden left Elkton Hills, Mr Antolini has continued to take an interest in him and has dined with the Caulfield family on several occasions.

Holden telephones Mr Antolini late at night from his parents' home and is immediately invited over to the apartment he shares with his wife. They have spent the evening entertaining friends and have just gone to bed, but do not mind being disturbed. Mrs Antolini prepares coffee and food before retiring again while Mr Antolini stays up to talk to Holden.

At first Mr Antolini is friendly and humorous, but his tone becomes more serious when he begins to talk about Holden's future. His advice to Holden is constructive and shows a sympathetic understanding of his disillusionment, which he fears will become total if Holden does not find some purpose and direction. Mr Antolini is a man of culture and considerable intellect and, unsurprisingly, he urges Holden to devote more time to academic study. He feels that through learning about the past Holden will realize that others too have been 'confused and frightened and even sickened by human behaviour' (p. 196) and that reading of their experiences may help him to overcome his own despair. Unfortunately Holden is too exhausted to absorb much of what Mr Antolini says. In any case, a suggestion that he take his education more seriously is unlikely to appeal to Holden, who has a deep-rooted aversion to school.

Holden's stay with Mr Antolini ends on an unhappy note when Holden wakes to find him stroking his head. Frightened and repelled by Mr Antolini's apparent homosexuality, Holden leaves his apartment as quickly as possible. The episode is significant because it destroys Holden's faith in one of the few adults he held in high regard and therefore reinforces his views of adult society.

Mr SPENCER

Mr Spencer is another teacher who is liked by Holden, but he is a more conventional figure and as a result Holden enjoys a less close relationship with him. He believes in established values and does not have Mr Antolini's insight into Holden's state of mind.

He is a kind man, and he and his wife regularly entertain Holden and other Pencey Prep students at their house. When Holden calls to say goodbye to him, Mr Spencer, like Mr Antolini, tries to offer him advice. He does not realize that Holden's lack of academic commitment is indicative of a wider frustration and apathy. He asks Holden if he has given any thought to his future and deliberately embarrasses him by reading his history examination paper aloud, hoping this will impress upon him the need for improvement. But Mr Spencer's attempts to communicate with Holden inevitably fail because, as Holden observes, 'we were too much on opposite sides of the pole' (p. 19). Mr Spencer accepts the social and educational system that Holden rejects. Holden tells Phoebe, 'Even the couple of *nice* teachers on the faculty, they were phonies, too' (p. 174). He goes on to describe how Mr Spencer would laugh ingratiatingly whenever the headmaster, Mr Thurmer, cracked a joke.

Mr Spencer's old age further alienates him from Holden. He has a stooped posture and when he dropped a piece of chalk in class, one of the students had to pick it up for him. Holden sometimes wondered 'what the heck he was still living for' (p. 11). When Holden visits him, he is dressed in a bathrobe and Holden admits to the reader that he always finds old men's bodies unpleasant to look at. His room smells of medicine and he is surrounded by pills. 'I'm not too crazy about sick people,' Holden confesses (pp. 11–12). Holden's attitude to Mr Spencer indicates that old age is another aspect of adult life he finds difficult to accept.

None the less Holden appreciates Mr Spencer's kindness and concern and is polite to him throughout their conversation. He feels sad when he finally takes his leave and he asks Mr Spencer not to worry about him. The fact that Holden wanted to say goodbye to Mr Spencer shows his affection for him and illustrates his considerate nature.

WARD STRADLATER

Ward Stradlater is Holden's room-mate at Pencey Prep. He is an energetic character who always appears to be in a hurry, and he comes bustling into the room when Holden is talking to Robert Ackley (p. 29). He has a good physique and is vain about his appearance. Holden says he 'was madly in love with himself' (p. 31) and 'spent around half his goddam life in front of the mirror' (p. 37). He is very much wrapped up in his own affairs and when Holden speaks to him, he pays little attention to what he says. He expects Holden to lend him his jacket and write a composition for him. He is, however, generally friendly and good-natured, and when Ackley criticizes him, Holden says in his defence, 'Stradlater's all right ... You don't know him, that's the trouble' (p. 28).

Holden is rather jealous of Stradlater's strength and masculinity, commenting on his 'heavy beard' (p. 29) and 'damn good build' (p. 30). He also envies Stradlater's sexual confidence, which contrasts with his own uncertainty and inexperience. This partly explains Holden's reaction when he learns that Stradlater is going out for the evening with Jane Gallagher. He is resentful of Stradlater's having a date with someone who used to be his own girlfriend. More importantly, however, he sees the experienced Stradlater as a threat to Jane's innocence, for Stradlater is a 'sexy bastard' (p. 38) who is unscrupulous with girls. On Stradlater's return Holden's fear and resentment explode and he launches a violent physical attack on his room-mate. Stradlater, who is much the stronger of the two, reacts with commendable restraint, but when his attempts to calm Holden down fail, he knocks him to the floor.

ROBERT ACKLEY

Robert Ackley, another pupil at Pencey Prep, is ostracized by the other boys. He was always referred to as 'Ackley', never by his first name or even by a nickname. His unpopularity is understandable in view of his repugnant personal habits and insensitivity towards others. He never brushes his teeth and rarely changes his socks. When he visits Holden's room, he cuts his fingernails and allows the clippings to fall on the floor. He does not show any real friendliness towards Holden. When he comes in, he says, 'Hi' as though he were 'terrifically bored' (p. 23) and when Holden asks if he wants to go with him to Agerstown for the evening, he gives the impression he is doing Holden a great favour by accepting the invitation. In Holden's room he moves Holden's and Stradlater's possessions around and ignores the fact that Holden is trying to read.

Holden says that Ackley had a 'terrible personality' and was 'also sort of a nasty guy' (p. 23). He is clearly irritated by Ackley's behaviour and disgusted by his personal habits. Yet Holden is sorry for him: 'That guy had just about everything. Sinus trouble, pimples, lousy teeth, halitosis, crumby fingernails. You had to feel a little sorry for the crazy sonuvabitch' (p. 43). Holden shows his sympathy for Ackley by talking to him when he barges uninvited into his room and by inviting him to join him on his trip into Agerstown. Such behaviour is characteristic of Holden and illustrates his caring nature.

CARL LUCE

Carl Luce is three years older than Holden, who originally met him when they were both pupils at Whooton School. He is self-centred, pretentious and very conscious of his own image. It is significant that when Holden suggests having a drink together, Luce says they should meet at the Wicker Bar, a fashionable club where, according to Holden, 'the phonies are coming in the window' (p. 148). He wants to appear a sophisticated man of the world and tells Holden that his current girlfriend is an older woman, a sculptress who lives in

Greenwich Village. She is Chinese, and when Holden asks if this appeals to him, he replies, 'I simply happen to find Eastern philosophy more satisfactory than Western' (p. 152). He speaks condescendingly to Holden throughout their conversation, making it clear that he is bored by his company and considers him immature. Holden is in desperate need of companionship and when Luce says he has to go, he begs him to stay. Luce, however, is unmoved and leaves Holden alone in the bar.

Holden realizes that Luce is conceited and pretentious and admits that he does not like him. He respects his intelligence, however, and recalls, 'He had the largest vocabulary of any boy at Whooton when I was there' (p. 155). He is particularly impressed by his apparent knowledge and experience of sex. At Whooton Luce had been Holden's Student Adviser and would frequently give talks about sex to Holden and some of the other pupils. At the Wicker Bar Holden tries to explain his own confused feelings about sex in the hope that Luce can offer him advice. Luce, however, is absorbed in his own concerns and has no interest in Holden's problems.

THE NUNS

Holden meets the two nuns when he has breakfast at a railway-station sandwich bar. They tell him that they are schoolteachers and have come to New York from Chicago to teach at a convent school. Holden talks to them about the books he has studied in his English classes. He is relaxed in their company and 'enjoyed talking to them a lot' (p. 117). Even though he has little money left, he insists that they accept ten dollars for their charity collection and when they leave, he wants to pay their bill for them. He compares them favourably with other women he knows, such as his aunt and Sally Hayes's mother, who would dress up if they had to collect for charity and would soon become bored if nobody paid them much attention.

It is significant that, as a result of their vocation, the nuns are outside the normal adult world and are free from the phoniness and corruption Holden associates with it. He admires their gentleness and moral purity, which is inherent in their chastity. Holden meets the nuns very soon after his sordid encounter with the prostitute, and their sexual innocence helps to explain his regard for them.

SUNNY

Sunny comes to Holden's room at the Edmont Hotel after he accepts the liftman's offer of the services of a prostitute. She has a hard, unfriendly manner and resists Holden's attempts to make conversation. Holden asks Sunny about herself, but she does not want to waste time talking; she regards what is to take place in the hotel room as a business transaction. Her coldness and impatience highlight Holden's nervousness and inexperience, but she herself is not very old. Holden believes she is about his own age and when she uses the expression 'Like fun you are', he thinks she sounds more like a 'kid' than a prostitute (p. 99). She has lost her innocence at a young age, and it is characteristic of Holden that he should begin to feel sorry for her. When he imagines her buying her dress in a store and the salesman thinking she was just 'a regular girl', he feels 'sad as hell' (p. 100).

Holden is unable to go to bed with Sunny partly out of sheer nervousness but also because he cannot enter into a sexual relationship in which there is no warmth and affection. He wants to get to know Sunny before making love to her and her detached, businesslike manner unnerves him. He cannot regard their encounter as impersonally as she does. The episode thus offers further evidence of Holden's sensitivity and reveals much about his attitudes towards relationships.

Unfortunately for Holden, the sympathy he shows to Sunny is not reciprocated. She is angry when she leaves and later returns with Maurice to demand more money. While Maurice is threatening Holden, she takes five dollars from his wallet. Only then does she show a little compassion, asking Maurice to stop pushing Holden around.

MAURICE

Maurice, the liftman at the Edmont Hotel, arranges for Sunny to come to Holden's room. He tells Holden it will cost him five dollars, but later goes to his room, accompanied by Sunny, and demands another five. When Holden refuses to pay and becomes abusive, Maurice punches him and he falls to the floor. Maurice represents a side of life Holden has not encountered before — a side of life that is seedy, brutal and dishonest. Adult society has let Holden down once again, yet his compassion and humanity are such that they extend even to Maurice: at the close of the novel he says, 'I sort of *miss* everybody I told about . . . I think I even miss that goddam Maurice' (p. 220).

HOLDEN'S PARENTS

Holden's parents are remote, shadowy figures about whom very little is learned in the course of the novel. This in itself is significant, because it suggests that Holden does not feel very close to them. He fails to contact them after he leaves Pencey Prep since he is worried about how they will react to the news of his latest expulsion. It is obvious that Holden does not usually confide in them or turn to them when he is troubled. He feels much more affinity with his younger sister, Phoebe. Holden's alienation from the world of adults appears to be such that it is even evident in his relationship with his parents.

Holden shows some affection for his parents, however, particularly his mother. She has suffered from nervousness and depression since Allie's death and Holden feels guilty when he thinks of the effect his expulsion will have on her. She enters the novel briefly when she speaks to Phoebe after returning with her husband from a party (Chapter 23). She appears firm but kind; she tells Phoebe she should not smoke, inquires how she enjoyed her evening and asks for a goodnight kiss. Her underlying unhappiness is apparent when she complains of a splitting headache and Holden states that this occurs frequently.

Holden's father does not appear in the novel at all. He is a wealthy corporation lawyer who often invests money unwisely in Broadway shows. This may help to explain Holden's own carelessness with money, though Holden does not see his father as somebody to emulate. He rejects the notion of a conventional adult career and tells Phoebe he does not want to become a lawyer.

Themes

CHILDHOOD, ADOLESCENCE AND THE ADULT WORLD

In *The Catcher in the Rye* the innocence of childhood is contrasted with the often corrupt realities of adult life. Holden Caulfield, who is sixteen at the time of the events described in his narrative, is close to manhood, but it is a threshold that he is in many ways reluctant to cross. He appreciates the natural goodness of children and wishes it could be preserved; his experiences of the adult world confuse and sadden him.

When Holden leaves Pencey Prep and travels to New York, he moves from the enclosed environment of a boarding school to a noisy, crowded and tough urban society. He is surrounded by adults and often tries to be accepted as an adult himself, lying about his age to people he meets. But as he observes at first hand the behaviour and attitudes of his elders, Holden finds little he can admire. The adult world appears artificial, materialistic and degenerate. He feels contempt for the pretentiousness of theatre and nightclub audiences and is appalled at the importance so many attach to wealth and social status. The perverted behaviour of his fellow guests at the Edmont Hotel disgusts him and when he meets a prostitute there, he is chilled by her detached, unemotional manner. Holden feels little empathy with the adults he encounters and they in turn are often unable to understand him. His attempts at communication repeatedly fail. Bernice, one of the girls he dances with at the Lavender Room, responds to his efforts to start a conversation with cries of 'What?' and 'Wudga say?' (p. 75). When he tries to talk to a taxi driver about the ducks in Central Park, the driver 'looked at me like I was a madman. "What're ya tryna do, bud?" he said. "Kid me?"' (p. 64).

It is true that not all the adults Holden comes across are as uncomprehending as this, and not all of them are insincere or morally corrupt. Mr Antolini appears at first to be such an exception. He is respected by Holden and realizes the extent of Holden's anxiety and confusion. Holden's stay at his apartment, however, results in yet more disappointment when he makes what Holden thinks are homosexual advances. The two nuns Holden meets at Grand Central Station are certainly free from the moral failings he encounters elsewhere. He is moved by their kindness and admires their life of self-denial. But in a sense the nuns are not exceptions either, because by choosing to reject worldly ambitions and desires they have deliberately placed themselves outside conventional society.

The prospect of adulthood fills Holden with doubts and apprehensions. Even the physical process of ageing repels him. He sometimes wonders why Mr Spencer carries on living and he finds the sight of his bare chest and legs under his bathrobe unpleasant: 'I don't much like to see old guys in their pyjamas and bathrobes' (p. 12).

There is an interesting disparity between Holden's view of the adult world and that of Sally Hayes, the girl who accompanies him to the theatre and the ice-rink. She is about Holden's age, but shares none of his depression and disillusionment, and Holden harshly condemns her. She accepts unquestioningly the values of her elders and is bewildered by Holden's savage denunciation of conventional attitudes (Chapter 17). For her the transition from adolescence to adulthood seems likely to be smooth and untroubled. The reader may find her enthusiasm for life refreshing when set against Holden's intense pessimism, but the novel suggests that she has this enthusiasm because her response to the world is shallow and unthinking.

Whereas Holden recoils from the physical decay and moral imperfection of adulthood, the contrasting freshness and innocence of children hold a strong attraction for him. He enjoys talking to children, is amused by their behaviour and believes most are naturally 'nice and polite' (p. 125). He is relaxed in their company, as may be seen when he is with the young girl in the park (Chapter 16) and the two boys in the museum (Chapter 25). The people for whom Holden has the highest regard are almost all children: Allie, Phoebe and Jane Gallagher, who to Holden is still a child rather than the adolescent she has now become. Phoebe is also the character with whom he finds it easiest to communicate; he believes she understands him and she 'always listens when you tell her something' (p. 174).

Holden wishes that the innocence of children could somehow be preserved. At the museum he is saddened to think that Phoebe's character is altering and that every time she visits the building with her classmates she will be slightly different. He would like the qualities of childhood to be as unchanging as the exhibits in the museum. This attitude is further illustrated by his catcher in the rye fantasy.

In the later chapters of the novel Holden appears to be moving towards an acceptance of the passing of time and the inevitable loss of innocence that accompanies it. As he walks through the park to the museum (Chapter 16), he recalls with pleasure his regular visits there when he was a pupil at Phoebe's school. When he reaches it, however, he finds he has no desire to go inside. Holden cannot explain this, but his decision not to enter the museum implies an awareness that his childhood is over: he cannot return to the past. More importantly, when he later watches Phoebe reaching for the gold ring of the merry-go-round, he knows that he must allow her to risk falling rather than intervene to protect her. In the final chapter of the novel Holden admits that he does not know what the future holds for him, but he has learned much from his experiences and is now better equipped to face the realities of adulthood.

SCHOOL

Holden begins his narrative on the day he leaves Pencey Prep. He is about to be expelled for consistent lack of effort and for failing examinations in four of his five subjects. From his conversation with Mr Spencer (Chapter 2) it emerges that he has had similar experiences at other schools. In the course of the novel it becomes clear that Holden's lack of educational success is caused less by laziness or limited academic ability than by a refusal to conform to a system ased upon values he finds it impossible to share.

encey Prep demands a commitment to the life of the school that n is unable to make. In the opening chapter the school is playing its annual football game against Saxon Hall. This was 'a very big deal around Pencey. It was the last game of the year, and you were supposed to commit suicide or something if old Pencey didn't win' (p. 6). Holden, however, has little interest in the game. He does not watch it from the grandstand, even though 'practically the whole school except me was there' (p. 6), but from a nearby hill, and he leaves before the game has finished. His alienation is confirmed by the fact that he has no close friends at the school. He tells no one when he decides to leave a few days early, and his parting cry to the other pupils in his dormitory is '*Sleep tight, ya morons!*' (p. 56).

Holden sees Pencey Prep as being riddled with hypocrisy and pretence. This 'phoniness' is typified by the advertisements for the school, which show a young man riding a horse and boast, 'Since 1888 we have been moulding boys into splendid, clear-thinking young men' (p. 6). Holden caustically observes that he has never set eyes on a horse during his time at the school and the few people he has met who might be described as splendid and clear-thinking must have been like that before they came to Pencey. Holden is also contemptuous of the serving of steak every Saturday, which he sees as a transparent attempt to impress parents who come to visit their sons on Sunday and ask what they had for dinner the previous night. Other schools Holden has attended have been similar. At Elkton Hills, for example, he felt 'surrounded by phonies' (p. 18). When the headmaster met visiting parents he would make sure he spent more time with those who appeared wealthy and important.

Holden also dislikes other aspects of school life, as he explains to Phoebe (Chapter 22) and Sally Hayes (Chapter 17). He speaks of the unhealthy, claustrophobic atmosphere of a boys' boarding school, where 'all you do is talk about girls and liquor and sex all day' (p. 137). The boys form themselves into cliques from which other pupils are ruthlessly excluded. At Pencey Prep 'they had this goddam secret fraternity that I was too yellow not to join' (p. 174). Robert Ackley was not allowed to be a member simply because 'he was boring and pimply' (p. 174). At Elkton Hills one bullying incident actually caused the victim, James Castle, to commit suicide. Holden disapproves of the way in which the educational system is used to promote social conformity, encouraging an acceptance of the materialistic values of the adult world: 'all you do is study, so that you can learn enough to be smart enough to be able to buy a goddam Cadillac some day' (p. 137).

As this quotation suggests, Holden's rejection of the schools he has attended is part of a wider dissatisfaction with society as a whole. Society's faults – such as materialism, cruelty and hypocrisy – are reflected in its educational institutions.

LOVE, SEX AND RELATIONSHIPS

Relationships with girls give Holden pleasure but also cause him much anxiety and confusion. As with other areas of life, he finds that his own attitudes and principles appear to conflict with those of the people around him, both adults and contemporaries.

Holden finds it particularly difficult to decide upon a clear and consistent attitude towards sex, admitting, 'Sex is something I just don't understand. I swear to God I don't' (p. 67). He is anxious to lose his virginity, but is too sensitive to have a purely sexual relationship with a girl. He explains to Carl Luce, 'I can never get really sexy – I mean *really* sexy – with a girl I don't like a lot. I mean I have to *like* her a lot. If I don't, I sort of lose my goddam desire for her and all' (p. 153). Holden is also reluctant to force his attentions on anyone who appears not to want them: 'The thing is, most of the time when you're coming pretty close to doing it with a girl – a girl that isn't a prostitute or anything, I mean – she keeps telling you to stop. The trouble with me is, I stop . . . The trouble is I get to feeling sorry for them' (p. 97). Although Holden is frustrated by his inability to make love to a girl he does not like or who is unwilling, his attitude earns the respect of the reader.

Holden tries to clarify his thoughts on sex by inventing rules for himself. He resolved 'to quit horsing around with girls that, deep down, gave me a pain in the ass' (p. 66). This reflects his desire not to become involved with girls he does not respect. He admits, however, that he broke the rule on the very day it was first formulated, and in the course of the novel he enters into a number of relationships that contradict his own principles. None of these is successful. His association with Sally Hayes, for example, inevitably ends in discord. He finds her stunningly attractive but dislikes her personality and considers she is a pretentious 'phoney'. She is much more conventional than Holden, and he finally realizes their incompatibility during their argument at the ice-rink, at the end of which they 'both hated each other's guts' (p. 139). His encounter with Sunny, the prostitute, is also a failure. Before he meets her, he thinks of Sunny not as a person but as someone who will enable him to lose his virginity: 'I figured if she was a prostitute and all, I could get in some practice on her, in case I ever get married or anything' (p. 97). But when she arrives in his room, Holden's natural humanity asserts itself and he finds himself feeling sorry for her. Sunny herself is cold and offhand, but Holden cannot share her detachment. He feels no sexual desire for her: 'I felt more depressed than sexy, if you want to know the truth' (p. 101).

The adult world does not help Holden to overcome his confusion over sex. At the Edmont Hotel he watches from his window the strange behaviour of some of the other guests: he sees one man dress up in women's clothing and in another room a couple are squirting water out of their mouths at each other. Holden finds a certain fascination in such activities, but also considers them degrading. He believes that relationships should be founded upon mutual respect: 'I think if you don't really like a girl, you shouldn't horse around with her at all, and if you *do* like her, then you're supposed to like her face, and if you like her face, you ought to be careful about doing crumby stuff to it, like squirting water all over it' (p. 66). Holden hopes that Carl Luce, an older youth who claims to have lost his virginity at the age of fourteen, will be able to offer him advice, but Luce is arrogant and self-centred and has no interest in Holden's problems.

It is significant that the relationship to which Holden attaches most value is one of companionable affection in which sex played no part: that with Jane Gallagher. Holden retreats from his confusion over his own sexuality into nostalgic recollections of the innocent summer he spent with Jane, sitting on her front porch playing checkers, holding hands at the cinema. Although Holden felt very close to Jane, they 'never necked or horsed around much' (p. 84). He would like to see her again, but the novel implies that such a relationship is no longer possible for Holden now that his childhood is past. It has become an unattainable ideal: Jane has grown up and is dating the experienced Ward Stradlater, and Holden's attempts to telephone her are unsuccessful.

NEW YORK

Most of Holden's narrative relates to the three days he spent in New York following his decision to leave Pencey Prep. One of the novel's strengths is the realistic description of its New York setting. Salinger creates a vivid impression of a crowded, bustling city. As Holden moves around the town he makes precise references to streets and districts: Greenwich Village, Broadway (thronged with people on their way to the cinema), Madison Avenue, Seventy-first Street (where Holden's family live), Sutton Place (where the Antolinis have their apartment), Fifty-fourth Street, Fifth Avenue (crowded with Christmas shoppers) and Lexington Avenue. The various hotels and night-spots Holden visits, such as Ernie's nightclub, the sleazy Edmont Hotel and the fashionable Wicker Bar, are brought convincingly to life. Other locations include Grand Central Station, the Museum of Natural History and Radio City with its ice-rink and music-hall.

The atmosphere of a city depends greatly upon its inhabitants, and as Holden roams through New York, he meets a wide variety of characters: aggressive taxi drivers, drunks who ask him the way to the subway, waiters who won't serve him alcoholic drinks and, at Ernie's, waiters who will. He has an unpleasant encounter with the criminal side of the city when he accepts the offer of a prostitute and is subsequently beaten up and robbed of five dollars. In contrast Ernie's is crowded with college students and the Wicker Bar is full of would-be sophisticates.

Although Holden lives in New York and can find his way around with ease, he appears alienated from the life of the city. He pours scorn on the pretentiousness of many of its inhabitants and disapproves of their materialism: 'In New York, boy, money really talks' (p. 73). He tells Sally Hayes, 'I hate living in New York' (p. 136) and tries to persuade her to run away with him. He wants to leave the artificial environment of the city and live close to nature: 'we could live somewhere with a brook and all . . . I could chop all our own wood in the winter-time' (p. 138).

Of course, Holden is alienated not just from New York but from society – or, more specifically, adult society – as a whole. This isolation is most tellingly evoked when he wanders alone and lost through Central Park (Chapter 20). Here the setting is used to give a powerful impression of Holden's psychological state. The desolation of the park – the cold, the darkness and the frozen lake – underlines Holden's loneliness and despair.

Style and Narrative Technique

STYLE

In *The Catcher in the Rye* J. D. Salinger succeeds in making Holden Caulfield sound like an authentic American teenager. His manner towards the reader is relaxed, casual and informal, and his language is peppered with slang expressions. The novel's conversational style is evident both in its vocabulary and in the construction of its sentences. Colloquialisms such as 'damn', 'goddam', 'swell', 'crazy' and 'helluva' are used repeatedly. Holden's vocabulary is limited and he relies heavily on certain words. He finds it difficult to articulate his despair and usually describes himself as 'sad', 'lonesome' or 'depressed', while people he dislikes are often 'phoney' and 'stupid'. When something pleases him, he says 'That killed me.' Sometimes words fail him almost completely and he uses expressions that are virtually meaningless: 'and all', 'sort of', 'or something'.

Sentences have a corresponding looseness and simplicity of construction. Often they are very brief: 'I was sort of hungry. While I was in the cab, I took out my wallet and sort of counted my money. I don't remember exactly what I had left, but it was no fortune or anything. I'd spent a king's ransom in about two lousy weeks. I really had. I'm a goddam spendthrift at heart. What I don't spend, I lose' (p. 113). When Holden employs longer sentences, their structure is not complex or sophisticated; rather the impression is of a rapid, uncoordinated series of thoughts, as when he speaks to Sally Hayes (p. 136):

'I hate living in New York and all. Taxi-cabs, and Madison Avenue buses, with the drivers and all always yelling at you to get out at the rear door, and being introduced to phoney guys that call the Lunts angels, and going up and

down in elevators when you just want to go outside, and guys fitting your
pants all the time at Brooks', and people always –'

The novel derives much of its power from the directness and
simplicity of its prose style. Holden's narrative retains the interest of
the reader because it possesses clarity, energy and authenticity.
His descriptions of people and events are frequently witty and
memorable:

You could see the whole field from there, and you could see the two teams
bashing each other all over the place. You couldn't see the grandstand too
hot, but you could hear them all yelling, deep and terrific on the Pencey side,
because practically the whole school except me was there, and scrawny and
faggy on the Saxon Hall side, because the visiting team hardly ever brought
many people with them.   (p. 6)

Then she introduced me to the Navy guy. His name was Commander Blop or
something. He was one of those guys that think they're being a pansy if they
don't break around forty of your fingers when they shake hands with you.
                                                                (p. 91)

Holden's distinctive voice inevitably dominates, but the contrasting
speech habits of the people he meets give the novel variety and reveal
much about each character. Mr Spencer's tone is formal and
schoolmasterly: 'Do you feel absolutely no concern for your future,
boy?' (p. 18). Mr Antolini's speech reflects his intelligence but is also
a little pompous and self-consciously intellectual. The taxi driver who
takes Holden to the Edmont Hotel (Chapter 9) is curt and monosyl-
labic. Maurice, the liftman at the Edmont, has a hard and aggressive manner: 'All right, chief, let's have it. I gotta get back to
work' (p. 107). Sally Hayes is effusive and somewhat affected,
given to describing things as 'grand' and 'marvellous'. Carl
Luce is pretentious ('I simply happen to find Eastern philosophy more satisfactory than Western', p. 152) and patronizing ('Must
we go on with this inane conversation?' p. 152).

Holden himself often adjusts his manner of speech in response to
the different people and situations he encounters. He addresses his
fellow pupils at Pencey Prep with abrupt informality: 'How 'bout
sitting down or something, Ackley kid? You're right in my goddam
light' (p. 24). To Mr Spencer he is courteous and respectful: 'How's
your grippe, sir?' (p. 12). In New York he often tries to speak as if he

were an adult, and on the telephone to Faith Cavendish he puts on a 'mature voice', believing he sounds 'suave as hell' (p. 68). He also tries to appear a man of the world when he meets Sunny, the prostitute: 'Allow me to introduce myself. My name is Jim Steele' (p. 99). With Maurice he wants to be seen as tough and unyielding: 'Why should I give her another five bucks? . . . You're trying to chisel me' (p. 107). These changes of tone help to suggest Holden's insecurity and uncertainty about the kind of adult he wishes to become.

NARRATIVE TECHNIQUE

Holden states at the beginning of the novel that his narrative will not take the form of a conventional autobiography. He will not begin by describing his parents and his early childhood and then go on to give a chronological account of his later years. Instead his story will recount the events of just a few days – the 'madman stuff that happened to me around last Christmas' (p. 5). Yet by the close of the novel the reader has learned much about Holden's past life and gained an intimate knowledge of his character. He discusses the other members of his family and his feelings towards each of them and tells of the death of his brother Allie and how he reacted to it. He recalls girl-friends, schools he has attended (and some of his teachers and fellow pupils), books he has read, plays and films he has seen. He also expresses his opinions on a variety of subjects, including money, sex, religion and war.

Rather than being presented in a logical, structured sequence, this information is given in the form of digressions from the main narrative. Holden repeatedly interrupts his story to air his views on some topic or to recollect a past event. These digressions are often only very loosely related to the immediate events of the story, but often they are of more importance: Holden's reminiscences of Allie in Chapter 5, for example, are more significant than the essay on Allie's baseball glove that he writes for Stradlater. The advantages of digression as a narrative technique are explicitly discussed when Holden tells Mr Antolini about Oral Expression, a course at Pencey Prep that required pupils to give talks to the other students (Chapter 24). If a boy deviated from his chosen subject, the rest were meant to shout, 'Digression!' at him. Holden had difficulties with the course because he likes it when somebody digresses. He says his attention is held when people talk about things that really interest them, even if this means that they wander away from their original subject. Earlier in the novel Holden says that one of his favourite authors is Ring Lardner, an American writer whose narrative style is, like that of *The Catcher in the Rye*, informal and loosely structured (p. 22). Holden also favours books which make the reader wish 'the author was a terrific friend of yours and you could call him up on the phone whenever you felt like it' (p. 22). This too is reflected in Holden's own tone towards the reader, which is relaxed and familiar.

Although we are encouraged to feel close to Holden, we should not lose sight of the fact that he is a fictional character. How far does his creator, J. D. Salinger, identify with his views? It has been said that Salinger's presentation of his central character lacks objectivity, and thus weakens the credibility of the novel. There is some truth in this. It is rather implausible that so many of Holden's experiences should provide justification for his pessimistic view of life. Holden's attitudes permeate the novel and alternative viewpoints receive only limited recognition. Often, however, Holden is plainly to be seen as immature, as when he invites a taxi driver to join him for a cocktail or when he confides his uncertainties about sex to Carl Luce. Ironically, it is someone much younger than Holden who points out the negativity of his response to life: his ten-year-old sister, Phoebe, who tells him, 'You don't like *anything* that's happening' (p. 176). That Salinger does not wholly endorse Holden's view of the world is suggested by the closing pages of the novel, in which Holden himself undergoes a change of attitude. He moves towards a recognition that children must be allowed to lose their innocence and an acceptance of human imperfection.

Glossary

Andover: distinguished American college

Annex: building added to a larger one

Arnold, Benedict: American soldier (1741–1801) who committed treason during the American War of Independence

atheist: person who does not believe in God

the axe: expulsion

The Baker's Wife: French film (*La Femme du boulanger*) made in 1938

BB gun: air rifle

Beowulf: epic poem in Old English

blasé: relaxed, sophisticated

boardwalk: wooden esplanade

booze hound: drunkard

bourgeois: middle class

brace: appliance for supporting a weak leg

Brooke, Rupert: English poet (1887–1915) particularly known for his First World War poems

Buick: type of car

bunk: nonsense

Burns, Robert: Scottish poet (1759–96)

butt: buttocks

can: lavatory

Canasta: card game

carousel: merry-go-round

Caucasians: members of the white race

château: castle or large country house in France

checkers: board game

chewed the rag: talked

chiffonier: chest of drawers

chisel: cheat

clavichord: keyboard instrument (Holden uses the word incorrectly)

clicks: cliques, small exclusive groups of people

closet: cupboard

Columbus, Christopher: Italian navigator (1451–1506) who discovered America

Cooper, Gary: American film actor (1906–61)

crocked: drunk

daiquiri: cocktail made of rum, lime juice and sugar

David Copperfield: novel written by Charles Dickens (1812–70)

Dickinson, Emily: American poet (1830–86)

Dinesen, Isak: pseudonym used by the Danish writer Karen Blixen (1885–1962)

Dixieland: style of jazz that originated in New Orleans

Donat, Robert: English actor (1905–58)

Douglas, Melvyn: American actor (1901–81)

exhibitionist: person who likes attracting attention to himself or herself

fall: autumn

falsies: padded bra

A Farewell to Arms: novel by the American writer Ernest Hemingway (1899–1961) *fencing meet:* fencing match

Ferdinand: Ferdinand II of Aragon, Spanish king who ruled jointly with his wife, Isabella, over various European territories in the late fifteenth and early sixteenth centuries

flits: homosexuals

flunk: to fail a test or examination

Flys Up: ball game

Fourth of July: day on which the USA celebrates its independence

fraternity: student organization for scholastic or extracurricular activities

furlough: leave of absence from duty

Gladstone: large travelling bag

glider: type of chair

gore: blood (usually clotted)

Grant, Cary: English actor (1904–86)

The Great Gatsby: novel written by the American writer F. Scott Fitzgerald (1896–1940)

Grendel: the monster in *Beowulf*

grippe: influenza

grools: people of gruesome appearance

haemorrhage: loss of blood from the blood-vessels

half-gainer: type of dive

halitosis: bad breath

Hardy, Thomas: English writer (1840–1928)

harrowing: acutely distressing

Harvard University: the oldest American college, founded in 1636

hatcheck girl: cloakroom attendant

highball: a drink of alcohol and soda served in a tall glass, usually with ice

hormones: substances that circulate in the body and affect the activities of cells

horney: hard

horn in: interrupt, intrude

horny: sexually aroused

hot-shot: person who is very successful or important

hound's tooth: textile pattern of broken checks

incognito: under a false identity

infirmary: hospital

Isabella: see Ferdinand

Ivy League: name given to eight prestigious universities in the eastern USA

janitor: caretaker

jitterbug: fast American dance, usually to the accompaniment of jazz music, popular in the 1940s

lagoon: shallow lake

Lardner, Ring: American writer (1885–1933)

latex: rubber

leukemia (Eng: leukaemia): form of cancer characterized by an abnormal increase in the number of white blood cells

loafers: casual shoes

'Lord Randal My Son': traditional ballad of unknown authorship

Lorre, Peter: Hungarian-born Hollywood film actor (1904–64)

lulu: thing or person that is outstandingly bad or good

Lunts: Alfred Lunt (1892–1977) and his wife, Lynn Fontanne (1887–1983), an American acting team

Maugham, Somerset: English writer (1874–1965)

minor: person who is under age

mitt: padded leather glove worn in baseball

muckle-mouthed: having a large mouth

mushy: sentimental

Navajo: the largest American Indian tribe

nickel: five-cent piece

nominate: to propose someone for election

nonchalant: cool, untroubled
N.Y.U.: New York University

Of Human Bondage: novel written by the English writer Somerset Maugham
Oliver Twist: novel written by Charles Dickens
oodles: plenty
ostracized: excluded from a social group

pacifist: person who is opposed to war
pedagogical: schoolmasterly
Princeton: prestigious American university
psychic: possessing supernatural mental powers
psychoanalysis: method of medical treatment in which a person's mind is examined
putrid: rotten, awful

qualms: feelings of uneasiness

Raimu: stage name of the French actor and comedian Jules Muraire (1883–1946)
ratty: wretched, unkempt
reciprocal: done in return
recuperating: recovering
The Return of the Native: novel by Thomas Hardy
Revolutionary War: war in which American colonies won independence from Britain (1775–82)
rile: annoy, irritate
rocks: jewellery
rubbering: looking around with great curiosity
rubbernecks: people who crane or twist their necks in curiosity and hence lack social polish

sacrilegious: offensive to something that is holy
sadist: person who enjoys inflicting pain

shoot the bull: talk
snowing: using flattery, persuasion
spendthrift: person who spends money wastefully
squaw: American Indian woman
Stekel, Wilhelm: Austrian psychoanalyst (1868–1940)
stiffs: dead bodies
suave: smooth, bland
swanky: smart

tail: a woman
tattersall: fabric with a pattern of checks
The Thirty-Nine Steps: film directed by Alfred Hitchcock (1935) and based upon the novel of the same name by John Buchan
Tom Collins: cocktail including gin, soda and lime or lemon juice
torso: the trunk of the body, excluding head and limbs
tossed his cookies: vomited
traits: characteristics
tumour: swelling
tuxedo: dinner-jacket

unscrupulous: unprincipled, without moral scruples

verification: proof
Vye, Eustacia: character in *The Return of the Native*

wad: roll of banknotes
West Point: United States Military Academy at West Point, New York
windbreaker: warm jacket with close-fitting neck, cuffs and waistband

Yale: prestigious American university
Year Book: annual school or college publication
Yogi: person who practises yoga

Ziegfeld Follies: American theatrical revue produced by Florenz Ziegfeld (1869–1932)

Discussion Topics and Examination Questions

DISCUSSION TOPICS

Your understanding and appreciation of the novel will be much increased if you discuss aspects of it with other people. Here are some topics you could consider:

1. To what extent does Salinger wish us to believe that Holden's pessimistic view of the society in which he lives is justified?
2. 'A mass of contradictions' – is this how you see Holden's attitudes towards relationships with the opposite sex?
3. 'Holden's vision of himself as the catcher in the rye confirms that he is an immature daydreamer.' Do you agree?
4. How far do Holden's problems appear to be resolved at the close of the novel?
5. Do you find Salinger's use of colloquial diction and his digressive narrative technique effective? What, if any, are the drawbacks of such an approach?
6. *The Catcher in the Rye* was published at the beginning of the 1950s. Is it still relevant to teenagers (and older readers) today?

THE GCSE EXAMINATION

In this examination you may find that the set texts have been selected by your teacher from a very wide list of suggestions in the examination syllabus. The questions in the examination paper will therefore be applicable to many different books. Here are some questions that you could answer by making use of *The Catcher in the Rye*:

1. In modern works of literature the central character is often someone who feels alienated from the society in which he or she lives.
   Choose a book you know in which this is the case and explain the reasons for the central character's feelings of alienation.
2. Choose a book in which the setting plays a particularly important part and explain the contribution that it makes to the overall impact of the story.
3. Many writers choose for their subject-matter the thoughts, feelings and experiences of a young person growing up and preparing to enter the adult world. Select a book which has such a theme and consider the author's treatment of it.
4. Writers often try to capture the variety of human nature in their work. Choose a book you know which has a varied range of characters and describe four of them, emphasizing the ways in which they contrast.
5. Select a book in which the central character's schooldays are described and discuss the author's presentation of them.
6. Many books or plays purposely leave the ending undecided or inconclusive. Write about a text where this might apply, explaining in this particular case whether you find such an ending satisfactory or not.

QUESTIONS ON *THE CATCHER IN THE RYE*

1. Discuss the theme of 'phoniness', with close reference to four characters or incidents.
2. Describe and compare the two schoolteachers who appear in the novel, Mr Spencer and Mr Antolini. How do their relationships with Holden differ?
3. 'The novel consistently contrasts childhood innocence and adult corruption.' Discuss this view of *The Catcher in the Rye*.

4. Describe three characters encountered by Holden during his time in New York and explain their importance to the novel.
5. What impressions do you form of Pencey Prep, the school Holden is attending at the beginning of his narrative? Why is Holden so unhappy there?
6. Describe and compare Holden's relationships with Jane Gallagher and Sally Hayes.

FOR THE BEST IN PAPERBACKS, LOOK FOR THE

In every corner of the world, on every subject under the sun, Penguin represents quality and variety – the very best in publishing today.

For complete information about books available from Penguin – including Pelicans, Puffins, Peregrines and Penguin Classics – and how to order them, write to us at the appropriate address below. Please note that for copyright reasons the selection of books varies from country to country.

In the United Kingdom: Please write to *Dept E.P., Penguin Books Ltd, Harmondsworth, Middlesex, UB7 0DA*

In the United States: Please write to *Dept BA, Penguin, 299 Murray Hill Parkway, East Rutherford, New Jersey 07073*

In Canada: Please write to *Penguin Books Canada Ltd, 2801 John Street, Markham, Ontario L3R 1B4*

In Australia: Please write to the *Marketing Department, Penguin Books Australia Ltd, P.O. Box 257, Ringwood, Victoria 3134*

In New Zealand: Please write to the *Marketing Department, Penguin Books (NZ) Ltd, Private Bag, Takapuna, Auckland 9*

In India: Please write to *Penguin Overseas Ltd, 706 Eros Apartments, 56 Nehru Place, New Delhi, 110019*

In Holland: Please write to *Penguin Books Nederland B.V., Postbus 195, NL–1380AD Weesp, Netherlands*

In Germany: Please write to *Penguin Books Ltd, Friedrichstrasse 10–12, D–6000 Frankfurt Main 1, Federal Republic of Germany*

In Spain: Please write to *Longman Penguin España, Calle San Nicolas 15, E–28013 Madrid, Spain*

In France: Please write to *Penguin Books Ltd, 39 Rue de Montmorency, F-75003, Paris, France*

In Japan: Please write to *Longman Penguin Japan Co Ltd, Yamaguchi Building, 2–12–9 Kanda Jimbocho, Chiyoda-Ku, Tokyo 101, Japan*

FOR THE BEST IN PAPERBACKS, LOOK FOR THE

PENGUIN PASSNOTES

This comprehensive series, deisgned to help GCSE students, includes:

SUBJECTS
Biology
Chemistry
Economics
English Language
Geography
Human Biology
Mathematics
Modern Mathematics
Modern World History
Narrative Poems
Nursing

SHAKESPEARE
As You Like It
Henry IV Part I
Henry V
Julius Caesar
Macbeth
The Merchant of Venice
A Midsummer Night's Dream
Romeo and Juliet
Twelfth Night

LITERATURE
Across the Barricades
Arms and the Man
Billy Liar
Cider with Rosie
Great Expectations
Gregory's Girl
I am the Cheese
Jane Eyre
Joby
Journey's End
Kes
Lord of the Flies
A Man for All Seasons
The Mayor of Casterbridge
My Family and Other Animals
Pride and Prejudice
The Prologue to the Canterbury
    Tales
Pygmalion
Roots
Saint Joan
She Stoops to Conquer
Silas Marner
To Kill a Mockingbird
War of the Worlds
The Woman in White
Wuthering Heights
Z for Zachariah